MW00774955

New Testament Holiness

BY
Thomas Cook

First Fruits Press
Wilmore, Kentucky
c2016

New Testament holiness.
By Thomas Cook.

First Fruits Press, ©2017
Previously published by Epworth Press, 1902.

ISBN: 9781621717461 (print), 9781621717478 (digital), 9781621717485
(kindle)

Digital version at http://place.asburyseminary.edu/
firstfruitsheritagematerial/154/

First Fruits Press
B.L. Fisher Library
Asbury Theological Seminary
204 N. Lexington Ave.
Wilmore, KY 40390
http://place.asburyseminary.edu/firstfruits

Cook, Thomas, 1867-1913
  New Testament holiness/ by Thomas Cook. -- Wilmore, Kentucky: First
Fruits Press, ©2016.
          158 pages; 21 cm.
          Reprint. Previously published: London: Epworth Press, 1902.
          ISBN - 13: 9781621717461 (pbk.)
          1. Holiness. I. Title.
BT767.C63 2016   248.4

Cover design by Jon Ramsay

asburyseminary.edu
800.2ASBURY
204 North Lexington Avenue
Wilmore, Kentucky 40390

First Fruits Press
The Academic Open Press of Asbury Theological Seminary
204 N. Lexington Ave., Wilmore, KY 40390
859-858-2236
first.fruits@asburyseminary.edu
asbury.to/firstfruits

NEW TESTAMENT
HOLINESS

BY

THOMAS COOK

THE EPWORTH PRESS

(EDGAR C. BARTON)

25-35 CITY ROAD, LONDON, E.C.1

PREFACE

AT one of our Theological Institutions the students asked their Tutor in Theology to give them a definition of Scriptural holiness. The Professor replied that the holiness he found in the Bible seemed to him to be not so much a definite experience to be reached immediately, as ' an eternal approximation towards an unrealizable ideal '. ' But,' he continued, ' there is, beyond doubt, an experience attainable by faith, which some describe as holiness, and which has brought to many Christians a great spiritual uplifting so as to mark an epoch in their spiritual life. This was taught by Wesley and the early Methodist Preachers, and the teaching was intimately associated with the early successes of our Church.' He advised the students to make themselves familiar with the works of Wesley and Fletcher, and to use their own judgement as to which aspect of the subject they would preach, and concluded with this testimony : ' In my last Circuit an Evangelist conducted a series of Mission Services in the Church over which I had pastoral charge and emphasized the definite view of holiness which Mr. Wesley teaches, and urged the people to believe and enter in. Several of the most thoughtful members of my congregation were so greatly blessed that from that time their Christian life seemed to be on a higher plane. Because of this, I have never spoken other than respectfully of that form of teaching, though I have never been able to teach holiness in that way myself.'

The Evangelist referred to by the Tutor is the writer of this book. It contains the substance of the addresses which were so much blessed to the congregation mentioned, and which have been used of God to help Christian people into the higher Christian life in many parts of the world. Testimonies received from those who have been definitely helped and blessed are so numerous that no apology is needed for their publication.

May He who has condescended to bless so richly the spoken word, still more abundantly crown with His favour that which is written.

CONTENTS

	PREFACE	-	-	-	-	-	-	-	3
1.	BLAMELESS, NOT FAULTLESS	-	-	-	-	7
2.	HOLINESS AND TEMPTATION	-	-	-	-	12
3.	SIN NOT A NECESSITY	-	-	-	-	16
4.	THE DOUBLE NEED AND THE DOUBLE CURE	-	22
5.	THE NEW BIRTH AND ENTIRE SANCTIFICATION	-	27
6.	PURITY AND MATURITY	-	-	-	-	33
7.	THE PRESENT TENSE OF CLEANSING	-	-	-	40
8.	A GOD-POSSESSED SOUL	-	-	-	-	46
9.	PERFECT LOVE	-	-	-	-	-	52
10.	EVANGELICAL PERFECTION	-	-	-	57
11.	THE FULLNESS OF THE SPIRIT	-	-	-	64
12.	A LIVING SACRIFICE	-	-	-	-	70
13.	WALKING WITH GOD	-	-	-	-	76
14.	BEULAH LAND	-	-	-	-	-	82
15.	SOUL REST	-	-	-	-	-	88
16.	CHRIST'S LEGACY TO THE CHURCH	-	-	-	96
17.	JOY IN THE HOLY GHOST	-	-	-	-	100
18.	POWER FOR SERVICE	-	-	-	-	104
19.	VESSELS UNTO HONOUR	-	-	-	-	110
20.	CONSECRATION	-	-	-	-	-	119
21.	SANCTIFYING FAITH	-	-	-	-	-	124
22.	ADDRESS TO SEEKERS	-	-	-	-	131
23.	HOW TO RETAIN THE BLESSING	-	-	-	139
24.	THE ARBITER OF THE HEART	-	-	-	147
25.	TESTIMONY	-	-	-	-	-	151

'From long experience and observation, I am inclined to think that whoever finds redemption in the blood of Jesus—whoever is justified—has the choice of walking in the higher or the lower path. I believe the Holy Spirit at that time sets before him the " more excellent way ", and incites him to walk therein—to choose the narrowest path in the narrow way—to aspire after the heights and depths of holiness—after the entire image of God. But if he do not accept this offer, he insensibly declines into the lower order of Christians; he still goes on in what may be called a good way, serving God in his degree, and finds mercy in the close of life through the blood of the covenant.'—JOHN WESLEY.

CHAPTER I

BLAMELESS, NOT FAULTLESS

C. H. SPURGEON once wrote as follows : ' There is a point of grace as much above the ordinary Christian as the ordinary Christian is above the world.' Of such he says : ' Their place is with the eagle in his eyrie, high aloft. They are rejoicing Christians, holy and devout men doing service for the Master all over the world, and everywhere conquerors through Him that loved them.' The experience to which Mr. Spurgeon refers has been described as the higher life, entire sanctification, Christian perfection, perfect love, the rest of faith, and by numerous other names or terms. Modes of expression have been selected by various Christians which have best coincided with their theological views. There may be shades of difference in their import, but, generally speaking, the terms mean one and the same thing. We do not contend for names. It is immaterial which expressions are employed; the main point is, do we possess the experience designated by these terms, and which is recognized and professed by Christians representing all our Churches? A profound and widespread interest has been awakened in this subject, and one of the most hopeful signs of the times is the obvious endeavour which is being made by teachers of various schools of thought to preserve the ' unity of the spirit ', and harmonize any conflicting view which may remain.

When used in a general sense, the word ' holiness ' includes whatever is connected with Christian life and character. Thus interpreted, it may be applied to any and all stages of religious life and development. But the term is used in a more definite sense to describe an experience distinct from justification—a sort of supplemental conversion, in which there is eliminated from the soul all the sinful elements which do not belong to it, everything anta-

gonistic to the elements of holiness implanted in regeneration. It includes the full cleansing of the soul from inbred
sin, so that it becomes pure or free from sinful tendency.
Says Thomas Carlyle: 'Holy in the German language—
Heilig—also means healthy; our English word whole—all
of one piece, without any hole in it—is the same word.
You could not get any better definition of what holy really
is than healthy, completely healthy.' We do not say that
this definition embraces all that we mean by holiness—it
does not. The experience includes also the gracious endowment of perfect love, and the abiding fullness of the Holy
Spirit. To explain more in detail in what sense the Scriptures teach this to be a present duty and privilege and to
meet the difficulties of those who really and honestly desire
to understand the doctrine, is our purpose in these pages.
To hit a mark we must know where it is. We walk faster
when we see plain, definite steps. We must know what we
want, and seek that. Unless we can separate the experience
from its accidental surroundings, confusion is sure to follow.
We may not be able to understand the doctrine in all its
relations and bearings, but we need to have before our
minds some distinct point of attainment. Just as the
pressing of men to an immediate and definite point of conversion produces immediate and definite results, so it is with
Christians. When a definite point is presented as immediately attainable, distinct and definite experiences follow.
Prayer is no more at random. The blind man cried for
'mercy', but 'mercy' was too general a prayer. Jesus
wanted to know what special kind of mercy the man
desired. When he asked for mercy which took the form of
the gift of sight, that special bestowal was granted.

It will help us to understand what holiness is if we
mention a few things which are often mistaken for it. It is
told in the life of Tauler that a layman, rich in the grace of
God, who had heard him preach, asked him, 'Sir, I beg
you for God's sake to preach us a sermon showing us how
a man may attain to the highest and utmost point it is
given to us to reach in this present time.' Tauler's discourse

giving his answer was in twenty-four divisions. All who seek the highest degree of holiness feel that there must be limitations. To be holy is to be

BLAMELESS, BUT NOT FAULTLESS

Grace does not make men infallible. Sin has so perverted our moral and spiritual powers, that we shall never in this present life be free from infirmities of human nature. Whatever our experience of the grace of God may be, the liability to error will cling to us until this mortal puts on immortality. Infirmities have their ground in our physical nature, aggravated by intellectual deficiencies. They are the outflow of our imperfect moral organization—the scars of sin which remain after the wound has been healed. Smallpox may be healed, but it leaves its mark. A cut limb may be cured, but the scar remains for ever. The pitcher of our human nature, which was broken when Adam fell, may be put together again, but it will never have the true ring it had before it was broken. To regain that it must be handed over to the Potter to be ground to powder and entirely reconstructed. Then, when death has reduced us to dust, and the Divine Potter has re-made us, body as well as soul, we shall be ' presented *faultless* before the presence of His glory with exceeding joy ' ; but ' until the coming of our Lord Jesus Christ ', all we can hope for is to be pre-served *without blame*.

Before his fall Adam was complete in his mental struc-ture, in the enthronement of his moral sense, and in the harmony and balance of all his faculties. He could reason rightly and always judge correctly, and therefore was adapted to the law of perfect obedience. He might be without fault, and because he might he was required to be so. But through lack of knowledge, defective memory, a fallible judgement, slowness of understanding, and numerous other infirmities, we are as liable to err as it is natural for us to breathe ; and every error is a breach of the perfect law which allows no deviation from perfect recti-tude. It is because it is impossible for us to keep the old

Adamic law—the law of innocence, or the Paradisaical law, as it is called—of which every mistake and infirmity is a breach, that we are placed under another law—the law of the second Adam, the Lord from heaven. This law is graciously adapted to our diminished moral and intellectual capacity, dwarfed and crippled as it is by original and actual sin. ' Love is the fufilling of the law.' ' Fulfil ye the law of Christ, the perfect law of liberty.' The only perfection possible on earth is a perfection of love, of motive, of intention. Our service of perfect love may be marred and defective, but God looks now not so much at what we do, as at what we intended to do. Given a pure and devoted heart, it is not so much successful achievement He looks for as right motives and intentions. If the *want to* sin is sin, may we not say that the purpose or the *want to* please God is accepted, even when we blunder and make mistakes? See that blind girl arranging strings across a sheet of paper. She wishes to write a letter to her father. By means of the strings she feels the way to keep as straight as possible. When the father receives that letter is he angry because here and there it is disfigured by a little blot or a crooked line? Of course he is not! He prizes that marred, defective writing of his blind child more than the most clerk-like communication of that week. He keeps it among his treasures. The perfection of it, in his eyes, is not the beauty of the well-formed letters or the cleanliness of the page, but the beauty of love, which just did its best to spell out its heart despite its blindness.

And again we say, God looks less at results than intentions. Perfect love is not always successful achievement; it is childlike purpose, *a sincere aim in all we do to please God*. Your child may make a blunder and need a lesson, but for all that, win a kiss, as the child who put her mother's boots into the oven to warm, that she might be comfortable when she went out. The boots were altogether spoiled, but what mother could blame her child whose intentions were so good? And this is how God weighs our actions. The world often blames His people when He does not. Those around us look at outward appearances; God looks at the heart. They see what we *do*; He sees *why* we do it. What a mercy it is He did not command us to walk before the world and be perfect! Walk before Me is the command; and all who love Him with a perfect heart, and thus know 'truth in the inward parts', are accepted of Him as fulfilling the law.

CHAPTER II

HOLINESS AND TEMPTATION

It is a mistake to suppose that there is any state of grace this side of heaven which puts a Christian where he *is* exempt from temptation. So long as a soul is on probation, it will be tested by solicitations to sin.

It is true, when the heart is cleansed from all evil, the warfare *within* ceases. The struggle with the flesh, or inbred sin, or depravity, by whatever name it may be called, comes to an end when all antagonisms to God are expelled from the soul, and Christ reigns without a rival. But there are other enemies than those which exist within, against whom we shall have to fight strenuously to the end. ' We wrestle not against flesh and blood, but against principalities, against powers, against the rulers of the darkness of this world, against spiritual wickedness (wicked spirits) in high places.' This implies temptation, but temptation cannot be inconsistent with holiness, because Jesus was 'in all points tempted like as we are, *yet without sin* '.

The Christian life is a long battle, but that fact does not imply that we are sinful, or inclined to sin. The nearer we live to God, the thicker and faster will Satan's arrows fly. Some Christians do not live near enough to God to be the subject of a downright spiritual struggle. There is no better evidence of grace and progress than that we are much harassed by Satan's emissaries. He does not need to employ his forces against nominal and inconsistent professors of religion. Severe temptation often precedes, or follows, special and signal blessing. Christ's great battle with Apollyon occurred immediately after the descent of the Holy Ghost at His Baptism. As soon as He had received the signal anointing, which was to prepare Him for His great mission, ' then was Jesus led up of the Spirit into the wilderness to be tempted of the devil ', His temptation was evidently a part of the Divine plan, not only permitted, but arranged for.   Experience was gained in His conflict with Satan, which could not have been obtained in any other way.   Having ' *suffered* being tempted ', He is now able to succour those who are tempted as would have been impossible had He not resisted Satan's fiery darts Himself.

Temptations are permitted for a purpose.   None can come without Divine permission.   Did not Satan complain that God had set a hedge about Job which he could not pass without a special permit?   The Indians say that when a man kills a foe, the strength of the slain enemy passes into the victor's arm.   In that weird fancy lies a great truth.   Each defeat leaves us weaker for the next battle, but each conquest leaves us stronger.

' Did Jesus Christ know that Judas was a thief?' was a question asked at one of our recent holiness meetings.   The reply was in the affirmative.   ' Then why did the Master, if He knew that, give him the bag?'   continued the interrogator.   The reply was as follows: God allows the bag to be put in every life—by the bag is meant that which is constantly testing our loyalty to Him—and usually the temptation comes in the weakest place of our character. God permits this because He knows we can only gain strength in the weak place by overcoming temptation at that point.   Each new triumph brings an increase of moral power, and makes victory the next time easier.   This is probably the reason why Bunyan places nearly all the great combats which Christian fought with Satan early in his journey.   The first years of Christian life are the formative period of Christian character when the assaults of the tempter are fullest of possibilities of benefit to the believer.

Samuel Rutherford writes: ' The devil is but a whetstone to sharpen the faith and patience of the saints.   I know that he but heweth and polisheth stones all the time for the New Jerusalem.'

Some sincere souls are in constant bondage because they have never been taught to discriminate between *evil thoughts* and *thoughts about evil*.   We must discern between things that differ.   So long as we are in this world, and so long as we have five senses coming in contact with a world abounding with evil, Satan will be sure to use these as avenues of temptation. But no taint comes on the spirit from temptation which is at once and utterly rejected. It may and should be instantly repelled.

Milton says:

> Evil into the mind of God or man
> May come and go, so unapproved, and leave
> No spot or blame behind.

It may seem difficult to some to ascertain whether certain states of the mind are the result of temptation, or the uprisings of the evil of their own nature. But when suggestions of evil awaken no response and kindle no desire, when they cause a shudder and a recoil, when they are opposed to our usual inclinations and desires, and cause pain, we may safely conclude that they are from without and not from within, and no self-reproach need ensue.

An evil thought springs from evil existing in the heart, but a thought about evil is a suggestion, flashed upon the mind by what we see or hear, or by the law of association, or by the enemy of our souls. Those who are holy have no evil within, consequently no evil thoughts; but intruding thoughts and whispers of evil will often need to be resisted. These are an unchangeable condition of probation. Provided proper caution has been used to avoid occasions of temptation, 'no spot or blame' is left behind, any more than the shadow of a cloud passing over a beautiful lake disturbs or defiles it. It is not temptation, but the yielding to it, that is sinful, and there is a condition in which we may, with St. Paul, always triumph.

Temptation is first presented to the intellect, flashed it may be in a moment, the thoughts are appealed to—this is the earliest stage of temptation. Thence it is transmitted to the sensibilities, in which region it operates upon the senses, appetites, passions, or emotions. There is danger lest these be excited with a desire for gratification. A critical stage of temptation is now reached, but no guilt is necessarily

contracted   In the case of those whose hearts are not
entirely cleansed from sin, the temptation finds more or less
inward sympathy, but there is no guilt incurred unless the
evil suggestion is cherished or tolerated.   The will has yet
to be challenged, and upon its decision depends entirely
whether the tempter is to be successful or not.   If the will
says ' No ' to the temptation, the tempter is foiled and
defeated, and the soul comes off more than conqueror.

Though it is possible for the fully-cleansed soul to listen
to Satan, and to reason with him until he again ejects sin
into the heart as of old—he ' beguiled Eve by his subtlety ',
whose heart was perfectly pure—still it is not so likely that
he will be successful as before the heart was cleansed from
sin.   There is no porter Parley within the citadel then, to
open the castle gates to the enemy who is without.   Holiness makes none so secure as that they cannot sin, but it
gives them to possess all the elements of strength and
stability.   Though the warfare be long and severe, yet, by
abiding in Christ, victory may be constant and complete ;
and as storms help to root the trees, we shall find that the
best helps to growth in grace are the affronts, the crosses,
and the temptations which befall us.

CHAPTER III

SIN NOT A NECESSITY

As explained in our last chapter, holiness does not bring exemption from temptation. It follows, therefore, that it is always possible for the entirely cleansed soul to sin. Holiness secures the safest possible condition on earth, but absolute security does not belong to this world.

Some assert that the doctrine of entire extirpation of sin from the heart puts the soul beyond real temptation. 'There can be no real temptation,' they say, 'to a soul which has nothing in its nature responsive to solicitations to sin.' But such an assumption is much too broad. It renders angels in probation, Adam in Eden, and our Lord Himself, incapable of real temptation. But the fact that some angels fell, that Adam sinned, and that Jesus Christ 'was in all points tempted as we are', should be sufficient proof that holy souls are capable of temptation.

If angels and Adam fell, we shall need to watch and pray, and keep our hearts with all diligence. Though it be true that we are less likely to sin when our hearts are pure, our attitude must always be one of self-distrust, of vigilant observation of our spiritual foes, and of unceasing carefulness lest we become 'entangled again in a yoke of bondage'. Eternal vigilance is the price of safety. Grace never induces presumption. 'Let him that thinketh he standeth take heed lest he fall.'

But while *inability* to sin does not belong to Christian experience, *to be able not to sin does.*

Capacity to sin is involved in the idea of accountability, but capacity does not involve necessity. There is grace available by which every regenerate soul, from the moment of regeneration, may go on in a career of victory, never falling into acts of sin.

Scripture, in revealing the future kingdom, tells us that here, in the earth-life only, shall we encounter sin. When all things are made new, and the Jerusalem, which is from

16

above, becomes the home of the holy, into it shall in no wise enter anything that defileth. Therefore with earth ends, for the Christian, the conflict with sin. How strange, if during this one awful solitary season of temptation, our Father should design for us a long-drawn-out, continuous, miserable defeat. Commanded to depart from all iniquity, yet in this sole arena of trial left hopelessly saturated with it! How opposed to such pessimistic thought is the experience which exclaims, ' Thanks be unto God who always leadeth us in triumph '!

Living without sin are words which shock many excellent persons, but how otherwise can the grand purpose of Christ's mission into the world be accomplished? He came ' to save His people from their sins '; but if Christians cannot be saved from sinning, if the teaching of the Westminister Catechism is correct, ' No man even by the aid of Divine grace, can avoid sinning, but daily sins in thought, word, and deed ', then the plan redemption is a failure.

The New Testament distinctly teaches that the salvation which Jesus has provided includes grace to live without sinning. What says St. Paul: ' Shall we continue in sin that grace may abound? God forbid. How shall we that are dead to sin live any longer therein?' And again, in writing to the Thessalonians, he says, ' Ye are witnesses, and God also, how holily, and justly, and unblameably we behaved ourselves among you that believe '. These were strong words for a mortal man to use—but they were true. The life he lived was declared by the Holy Ghost to be holy, and just, and unblameable. St. John's teaching exactly coincides with that of St. Paul. The purpose of his Epistles was to warn believers against sin, and to keep them from it. ' These things write I unto you, that ye sin not.' To any unprejudiced reader the whole teaching of the third chapter of his first Epistle is to the effect that as certainly as we may be saved from the consequences of sin by faith in Christ, so may we be kept from sinning by abiding in Him. Because they need not, Christians must not sin; the possibility involves the obligation. The

2

difference between Christians in a lower and higher state of grace is not that the one sins and the other does not. That is the essential difference between a sinner and a saint. ' In this,' says the apostle, ' the children of God are manifest, and the children of the devil.' Some say, ' This means habitual sinning,' but the Scripture does not say habitual sin. St. John spoke in God's name when he said, ' He that committeth sin ', that is, knowingly and willingly, ' is of the devil '. No state of grace permits the committing of voluntary sin. Even the lowest type of Christian does not continue in sin.

Another point is also made clear in this chapter, viz., that permanent sonship and continual sinning are contradictions which cannot be combined in the same character. A person can no more remain born of God and continue in sin, than he can remain honest and steal, or truthful and tell lies.

When a soul is born of God, a new principle (the love of God) is admitted, and takes up its abode behind the will. The attitude of the will can never be hostile to God's law, so long as it is swayed by love to the lawgiver. This interprets the declaration, ' Whosoever is born of God doth not commit sin, for his seed remaineth in him (this new principle of love) and he cannot sin, because he is born of God '. Such ' cannot sin,' in the sense that a dutiful son says ' I cannot ' when he is tempted to do his parents, to whom he is under deepest obligations, some great wrong. He cannot because he will not; the impossibility is not physical but moral.

There is truth in the saying—

> If we will we may, but if we won't we can't.

We recognize, of course, to some extent, a difference between sin committed as the result of momentary weakness or unwatchfulness, and that which is committed deliberately, with set purpose. In an unguarded moment, the best Christians may be surprised into some single act of sin ; but for this there is merciful provision in our High Priest above. But even these 'surprise sins', as they may be designated, are not a necessity. The *if* clearly implies they are not. '*If* any man sin, we have an Advocate with the Father.' What nonsense it would be to use this word if there were no room for a condition! How absurd it would be to say, ' If any man sin, for every man does sin! ' And how directly contrary to the tenor of the Epistle!

The Scriptural doctrine is undoubtedly this: Christians need not, and do not sin, but capability to sin remains. Should one be overtaken in a fault let him not despair. God, in His mercy, has made sufficient provision in Christ for his forgiveness and cleansing again, if he confesses the wrong he has done.

Much controversy about sin results from the want of accuracy in the definition of the term. We do not in this chapter understand by sin involuntary deviation from the law of absolute right, but willing transgressions of the known law of God. What is commonly meant by *committing sin,* in the New Testament, is a willing and known transgression of a known law We deny that unconscious and involuntary breaches of the Adamic law are sins. To a superficial observer they may seem like sins, but in lacking volition, they lack sin's essential characteristic. Sin is in the will and purpose rather than in the act. Ethical writers insist that guilt always involves a knowledge of wrong, and an intention to commit it. The moral sense of mankind pronounces innocent the inadvertent doer of an act wrong in itself. It discriminates between a sin, and a weakness or an error. And when we look into the Word of God we find this distinction always recognized. On the great day of Atonement, the errors (ignorances) of the people were put away through the blood which the High Priest offered for himself, and the errors of the people. (Hebrews ix. 7.) But where sin had been committed by the individual Hebrew, he needed to offer a special victim for himself. Sins demand a personal confession and personal resort to the blood of sprinkling, and an act of reliance upon Christ; but involuntary transgressions, so-called sins of ignorance, are covered by the blood of Christ without any definite act of faith on the part of the believer. In speaking of such involuntary transgressions, Mr. Wesley says, ' You may call them sins if you please, I do not. What is sin? Sin is the transgression of the law. But is all transgression of the law sin? Prove it who can.'

Evils arising out of unavoidable ignorance are certainly not sins in the sense of attaching guilt to the perpetrator. They are his misfortune, not his fault. Their penalty may be suffering, but it is not condemnation. If it were condemnation, we should always be in bondage, because we come short of God's absolute standard of right every moment of our lives.

It is true that all ignorances, infirmities, and mistakes need the atoning blood as much as sin does. However holy a man may be, if he thinks he can live a moment without the Atonement he is a mistaken man. To say that because our hearts are cleansed from all sin we do not need the Atonement, is as absurd to say because it is noon-day we do not need the sun. Even our best actions are so far short of God's absolute standard of right that we could not stand a moment if tried by the law as a covenant of works. We stand in grace alone—accepted only in Christ—every moment needing, and every moment enjoying the merit of His death. Apart from vital union with Him, we are required to keep the law of perfect obedience, as Adam was; but when in Him, so far as we come short, because of our imperfect moral organization, His merit meets our de-merit. ' Christ is the end of the law for righteousness to every one that believeth.' It is in view of this truth that the holiest soul on earth will always find that petition in the Lord's prayer appropriate, ' Forgive us our debts, as we forgive our debtors '.

Mistakes, infirmities, and involuntary offences are inevitable so long as we are in the body. Sins, by the keeping power of Christ, are avoidable throughout every hour of our regenerate life. He will so energize the will, that it shall be able to stand as flint against every suggestion to act

contrary to the will of God. No power on earth or in hell
can compel a man to sin who relies upon God to be kept
from it. Christ came not to cover over, make excuse for, or
give liberty to sin, but to give us uninterrupted victory, to
teach us that by continuous trust in Him we need never
know defeat. There is almost excess and extravagance of
victory implied in the word which the apostle coined to
express his experience, ' We are more than conquerors '.
Dr. Rendel Harris says : ' We should render it exactly by
saying, " we over-over-conquer ".'   Coverdale gives the
sense of it well in his translation, ' We conquer far '. This
is in exact harmony with the assurance, ' Where sin
abounded, grace shall much more abound '.

If man were left to himself we should all admit the thing
is impossible, but it is not a question of what *we* can do, but
of what *He* can do. ' Is anything too hard for the Lord ? '
Cannot we, by the grace of God, live one minute without
sin? If a minute, why not an hour? If an hour, why not
a day? If a day, why not a year? Shall we limit ' the
Holy One of Israel ' ? There can be no continuous victory
over sin unless such victory is expected, and no Christian
will expect what he believes cannot be experienced. We are
weak, but ' through Christ strengthening ' us, ' we are
able to do all things '.

' All things are possible to him that believeth.'

The most impossible of all,
　Is, that I e'er from sin should cease ;
Yet shall it be, I know it shall ;
　Jesus, look to Thy faithfulness !
If nothing is too hard for Thee,
All things are possible to me.

CHAPTER IV

THE DOUBLE NEED AND THE DOUBLE CURE

THE reason why many do not apprehend the true nature of
the salvation of Jesus Christ is because they do not understand the true nature of sin. Defective views of sin lead to
incorrect views of privilege. What we think of the Atonement depends greatly upon our view of the evil which made
it necessary.

Without the fullest information about sin, no man can
have the fullest information about himself; or, what is still
more important, without understanding sin no man can
ever understand God and His dealings with us. The man
who has felt his guilt most deeply always appreciates most
the value of Christ's redeeming work. Sin has many aspects,
but there are two primary forms in which it exists. We can
form no adequate conception of its nature, nor of the
remedy God has provided, unless we look at it from these
two points of view. We must discriminate between guilt
and depravity.

Sin is wrong-doing, but a state of sinfulness existed before
we began to do. Wrong-doing involves guilt, and needs
forgiveness, but a state of sinfulness cannot be forgiven.
Pardon refers to actions, but a sinful condition is not action.
Sin in the sense of guilt is a voluntary violation of the
Divine law, an actual transgression in thought, word, or
deed; but depravity is an involuntary state of the heart
which we have inherited from our first parents in the fall,
hence it is often described as *inbred* or inborn sin. Depravity is not actual sin, it is the inward fountain from
which actual sin originates; that inward cause of which
sins are the effect. It is deeper down and farther back in
our nature than wrong-doing. It is sin in embryo—that
state of the heart out of which acts of sin are born.

' A man is not a sinner,' says a late writer, ' because he
does evil; he does evil because he is a sinner. Train him
as you will, evil will come out of him if it is in him.'

Behind the doing of sin is the being of sin, and it is only by removing the cause that the effect will cease. The whole tenor of Scripture teaches that the purpose of the death of Christ was not merely to save men from the consequences of sin, but to save them from sin itself—the sin which causes the sins. It is this being, or ' body of sin ', as St. Paul terms it, that is to be ' crucified ' and ' destroyed ', in order that ' henceforth we may not serve sin ' (Rom. vi. 6). The Divine method is not to lop off a branch here or cut away an excrescence there, but to strike at the root.

We have read of a man who said he had cured his boy of pilfering, and on being asked how he had done it, he said he had tied his hands behind his back. It need scarcely be said that this is not the way in which God works. Hands do not steal, there is something behind the hands. Some will say there is the will, but our nature is behind our will, and it is there where we need to be put right. Better than his creed a man may be, but no man is better than his heart. The heart in the Word of God stands for condition, as distinguished from conduct. A man will *do* according to what he *is*. The heart is the spring from which issue the streams that make up the sum total of a human life. If the fountain be kept pure, all the streams will be pure. When the heart is right the outward life will correspond as naturally as fruit to a tree. Hence the exhortation, ' Keep thy heart with all diligence, for out of it are the issues of life '.

Does not the high import of the Sermon on the Mount consist in the fact that a moral condition is demanded antecedent to the act? Not only is the external observance of the ten commandments required, but the secret desires of the heart must be pure. Most persons have never committed the sin of murder as an act, i.e. they have never lifted their hand to strike the fatal blow ; but St. John teaches. ' He that hateth his brother is a murderer '—that those who cherish feelings of malice or desires for revenge are as certainly guilty as those who have committed the deed. The law is as surely broken by the man who would sin if he dared, as in the case of him whose state of heart finds expression in outward acts.

Depravity as such is not always seen in the outer life, but it is manifest to the painful consciousness of the believer. When he would do good evil is present with him. The strong man is bound, but not being cast out, he makes desperate efforts to burst his bonds and reassert his supremacy in the household. The evil within may be kept in subjection, but the struggle is often so severe and protracted that ever and anon the bitter cry is extorted, ' O wretched man that I am, who shall deliver me from the body of this death ? '

The penitent convicted of his sins seeks Divine forgiveness. The believer convicted of the depravity of his nature sighs for inward purity. The one inquires, How can the sins which are past be forgiven? the other asks, How can I be cleansed from conscious impurity? We are guilty for what we have done, but we were depraved before we were responsible for our doing. The existence of both original and actual sin has always been accepted by the Christian Church as a Scriptural doctrine.

It is because sin exists in this twofold character, as an act and as a state, that salvation assumes a twofold aspect, or is applied in two forms. For guilt there is forgiveness, for depravity there is cleansing, Forgiveness is complete forgiveness, but forgiveness can only extend to actual transgression. A mother puts upon her child a clean pinafore, and says, ' Now, this must not be soiled '. But the child disobeys. The mother may forgive the child for her disobedience, but she cannot forgive the pinafore clean ; she must wash it. So God may forgive the wrong we do, but He cannot forgive a depraved heart. Depravity is removed by purgation or cleansing. This is in perfect harmony with the Scriptures. Zechariah represents the fountain of Atonement as opened to meet this double need—pardon for sin (guilt), and purity for uncleanness (depravity). St. John's teaching is exactly the same. ' If we confess our sins, God is faithful and just to forgive us our sins (guilt),

and to cleanse us all from all unrighteousness (depravity).'
And with this view the hymn is in exact accord : —

> Let the water and the blood,
> From Thy wounded side which flowed,
> Be of sin the *double cure,*
> *Save from wrath, and make me pure.*

This twofold provision for the two forms in which sin
exists runs all through the Scriptures.   It was typified in
the history of God's ancient Israel when they crossed the
Red Sea and the Jordan in leaving Egypt and entering
Canaan.   We enter the holy place by regeneration, but let
us not forget that, *after the second veil* is the tabernacle
which is called the ' Holy of Holies ' (Heb. ix. 3).

We do not deny that in some instances Divine forgiveness and complete inward cleansing may have been experienced at one and the same moment, but certainly that
is not the usual order in which God works.   Both Mr.
Wesley and Dr. Adam Clarke inform us that they never
met with a single instance when God both pardoned guilt
and purified the heart at the same time.   The explanation
is that God's work is always in harmony with man's faith.
The work wrought and the blessing obtained are in accordance with the faith exercised.   God bestows what the
soul's intelligence perceives to be its need, and what faith
humbly claims.

The faith of the sinner seeking forgiveness is limited by
the view his intelligence takes of his necessity.   His all-
pervading desire is to be pardoned.   He is guilty, and must
be forgiven.   Every other thought is swallowed up in the
sense he has of his need of Divine mercy.   His prayer is,
' God be merciful to me, a sinner '.   It is this prayer God
hears and answers.   All his sins are forgiven, fully forgiven
for Christ's sake.   He receives according to his faith.

But as yet he knows little of the deep depravity of his
heart.   God graciously tempers His revelations of our need
to our weakness.   In like manner, He did not lead the
children of Israel by the shortest route into Canaan ; He
led them by a round-about way, lest they should despair in

view of the difficulties. It would paralyse the faith and extinguish the hope of many if they had revealed to them their inward corruption when they first see and feel their guilt and danger. Not until the soul can bear the revelation does the Spirit of God reveal ' the depths of inbred sin '. There is a conviction of our need of cleansing analogous to the conviction of guilt and danger which precedes our pardon and renewal. A painful sense of need is wrought when the Holy Spirit discovers to us the plague of our hearts, the abominations which lurk and fester within the chambers of our souls. Under His all-searching and piercing gaze, the sense of sin within becomes deeper and more poignant, until, deeply humbled we bewail our condition, and cry with the Psalmist, ' Create in me a clean heart, O God, and renew a right spirit within me '. It is then, when our intelligence apprehends the soul's deep need of inward purity, that definite prayer is offered, definite faith is exercised, and God speaks the *second* time, ' Be clean '.

To those who deny that there is any such second great work of grace, or crisis, which marks a distinct epoch in Christian life, we could commend the words of Dr. W. B. Pope, late of Didsbury College, Manchester. Speaking at a meeting for the deepening of spiritual life, he said :

' I have sometimes very delicately scrupled at this, that, and the other expression, and I have wondered whether it is right to speak of a " second blessing " ; and I have taken a text in which our Saviour takes a blind man and partially restores him his sight ; and then, holding the man up before us for a little while, that we may study his state, which is a great advance upon what it was, that we may watch him in this state of struggle between sin and the flesh, He touches him again, and he sees every man clearly. In the face of that text, and in the face of the experience of multitudes of our fathers, in the face of the testimonies of multitudes now living, and in the face of the deep instinct, the hope and desire of my own unworthy heart, I will never again write against the phraseology referred to.'

CHAPTER V

THE NEW BIRTH AND ENTIRE SANCTIFICATION

DIVINE forgiveness and the new birth are ever co-existent and inseparable. No man receives the new name of a child of God without at the same time receiving a new nature. He becomes there and then a partaker of the Divine holiness. Condemnation is removed, the culprit is forgiven, and as invariably as day follows night, a sublime change is wrought by the Holy Spirit, creating within the soul a new spiritual life, a life of loyalty and love.

The Scriptures describe this work of the Holy Spirit as a new creation, a being ' born again ', ' born of the Spirit '; a passing ' from death unto life ', ' quickened with Christ ', and by many like expressions all indicating newness and sanctity. It is such a renewal of the soul as turns the prepondering tendencies towards God; the love of sin is destroyed, the power of sin is broken, and a desire and relish for holiness is begotten.

In a measure and to a certain extent the Christian is sanctified when he is regenerated. He is set apart for God. He is made a new creature in Christ Jesus. A new and heavenly life is breathed into him by the Holy Spirit. He is translated out of darkness into marvellous light. The dominion of sin is broken. The love of God is shed abroad in his heart, which is the incentive to obedience, and the germ of holiness. His desires, tastes, impulses, aims, and aspirations are all changed. He no longer ' lives unto himself ', ' his life is hid with Christ in God '. He has victory over the world and sin, enjoys inward peace, walks before God in newness of life, and loving God, keeps His commandments.

Regeneration is holiness begun. Whatever is of the essence of holiness is found in germ in all who are children of God. But though all the elements of holiness are imparted the work of inward renewal is only begun, not finished, by regeneration. On this point there is harmony of faith among all the Churches. They hold that regeneration does not free the soul from depravity. It introduces a power which checks the outbreaking of depravity into actual sin, but inward corruption remains, manifesting itself in a bias towards evil, in inclinations to sin, in a proneness to depart from God, 'a bent to sinning'. Says Bishop Foster: 'Sin committed, and depravity felt, are very different: the one is an action, the other a state of the affections. The regenerate believer is saved from the one, and he has grace to enable him to have victory over the other; but the disposition itself to some extent remains, under the control of a stronger gracious power implanted, but still making resistance, and indicating actual presence, and needing to be entirely sanctified.'

It is by no means uncommon for persons to imagine at the time of forgiveness that depravity is completely destroyed. The change is so great, even as 'from death unto life', that the work of moral renovation seems perfect. The love and gladness of the newborn soul is so overflowing, as for a time to create the impression that the heart is entirely cleansed. 'How easily do they draw the inference, I feel no sin, therefore I have none; it does not stir, therefore it does not exist; it has no motion, therefore it has no being. But it is seldom long before they are undeceived, finding sin was only *suspended,* not *destroyed.*' When this occurs the new convert is often surprised and alarmed, and sometimes deems his conversion a failure, not knowing the Scriptures or the two-fold nature of sin.

'That a distinction exists,' says Richard Watson, 'between a regenerate state, and a state of entire and perfect holiness, will be generally allowed. Regeneration, as we have seen, is concomitant with justification, but the apostles, in addressing a body of believers in the Churches to whom they wrote their Epistles, set before them, both in the prayers they offer on their behalf, and in the exhortations they administer, a still higher degree of deliverance from sin, as well as a higher growth in Christian virtues. Two passages only need to be quoted to prove this:—

1 Thess. v. 23 : "And the very God of peace sanctify you wholly: and I pray God your whole spirit and soul and body be preserved blameless unto the coming of our Lord Jesus Christ." 2 Cor. vii. 1 : "Having therefore these promises, dearly beloved, let us cleanse ourselves from all filthiness of the flesh and spirit, perfecting holiness in the fear of God." In both these passages deliverance from sin is the subject spoken of ; the prayer in the one instance, and the exhortation in the other, goes to the extent of the entire sanctification of the "soul" and "spirit", as well as of the "flesh" or "body", from all sin; by which can only be meant our complete deliverance from all spiritual pollution, all inward depravation of the heart, as well as that which, expressing itself outwardly by the indulgences of the senses is called filthiness of flesh and spirit.'

In regeneration sin is subdued and conquered, but it is not destroyed. The fortress of Mansoul has been won for its legitimate Lord, but within its garrison some traitors lurk, mained and bleeding, but not dead. The disease is modified, but it is not eradicated. The bitter and baneful thing is nipped in the bud, some of the branches are lopped off, but the root is not removed. Depravity is suspended, held in check, repressed ; but it is not fully expelled from the soul. It does not reign, but it exists. Tendencies to sin are controlled, but they are not extirpated. There is still a warfare within, a sort of duality, in which flesh and spirit antagonize each other. It is a state of mixedness, in which Christians in a degree, according to the measure of their faith, are spiritual, yet in a degree they are carnal. We would not for a moment minify the great and glorious work of conversion, but all experience testifies that an 'infection of nature does remain, warring against the Spirit even in those who are regenerate'. The result often is that from the germ-sins in the heart spring actual sins in the life.

Regeneration is the beginning of purification. Entire sanctification is the finishing of that work. Entire sanctification removes from the soul all the elements which antagonize the elements of holiness planted in regeneration.

It is an elimination, as dross is separated from the gold by fire. It is an eradication, the removal of all roots of bitterness, the seeds of sin's disease. It is a crucifixion, the putting to death of the body or the life of sin. It is such a complete renewal of the heart that sin has no longer any place within, its last remains are scattered, the war within the citadel ceases and God reigns without a rival.

There are those who teach that entire sanctification consists in the power of the Holy Spirit repressing inbred sin, holding in check our sinful proclivities, choking down the old man instead of putting him to death. When the apostle speaks of *the body of sin being destroyed* (Rom. vi. 6) they tone down the meaning of the word *destroyed,* and explain it as meaning *to render inert or inoperative;* but Dr. Steele with his critical research points out the strength of the word by comparing it with the following texts where the *same word* is rendered ' abolish ', ' consume ', or ' destroy ' : 2 Corinthians iii. 13, Ephesians ii. 15, 2 Timothy i. 10, 1 Corinthians vi. 13, 1 Corinthians xv. 26, 2 Thessalonians ii. 8, Hebrews ii. 14. We have no fear of the result of a careful investigation of these texts by unprejudiced and candid minds.

The same writer also calls attention to the fact, that while the Greek language abounds in words signifying repression, a half-score of which occur in the New Testament, and are translated by *to bind, bruise, cast down, bring into bondage, repress, hinder, restrain, subdue, take by the throat,* yet none of these is ever used of inbred sin, but such verbs as signify to cleanse, to purify, to mortify or kill, to crucify, and to destroy. ' We have diligently sought,' he says ' in both the Old Testament and the New, for exhortations to seek the repression of sin. The uniform command is to put away sin, to purify the heart, to purge out the old leaven, to seek to be sanctified throughout spirit, soul and body. Repressive power is nowhere ascribed to the blood of Christ, but rather purifying efficacy. Now if these verbs, which signify to cleanse, wash, crucify, mortify, or make dead, and to destroy, are all used in a metaphorical sense, it is evident that the literal truth signified is something far stronger than repression. It is eradication, extinction of being, destruction.' Here is surely sufficient warrant for the prayer:—

> Every deed and thought unruly
> *Do to death;* for He has died.

This teaching is confirmed also by the prayer, already referred to, which St. Paul offered for the Thessalonians, ' And the very God of peace sanctify you wholly '. The word ' sanctify ' has two principal meanings: (1) to dedicate, or set apart, things or persons to sacred purposes; (2) to cleanse or purify. In the prayer before us the word is used in the latter sense, and to denote the thoroughness and pervasive nature of the purification prayed for, the apostle uses a strong word which is found nowhere else in the New Testament. Commentators agree that the word translated ' wholly ' is one of the strongest words that could possibly be used to express complete deliverance from spiritual pollution. Dr. Mahan says it is compounded of two words, one meaning *all,* the other *perfection.* Dr. Adam Clarke says the original word signifies precisely the same as our English phrase, ' to all intents and purposes '. Luther translates it ' through and through '. In the Vulgate it is rendered ' in your collective powers and parts '. Mr. Wesley says it means ' every part of you perfectly '. If full deliverance from sin is not taught in this prayer, it is not within the power of human language to teach it. Thrice welcome the assurance that follows the prayer : ' Faithful is He that calleth you, who also will do it.'

Do any ask what is the exact difference between regeneration and entire sanctification? It is this : the one has remaining impurity; the other has none. We do not say that entire sanctification embraces nothing more than complete cleansing from sin—it does. It is the full gracious endowment of perfect love, and much else, but with the positive aspects of holiness we will deal later. It is sufficient in this chapter to set forth the fact that entire sanctification completes the work of purification and renovation begun in regeneration.

The difference betweeen the two experiences has been well illustrated, as follows:—In the coal regions of the Wyoming Valley, in America, there are two principal seams of coal. In the first and upper seam there is a great preponderance of coal, but there are small seams of slate running through the coal. The lower seam of coal is much thicker than the upper seam, and it is all pure, solid coal, without any slate. The upper seam resembles the regenerate heart, in which there is a preponderance of grace, but there are also remains of the carnal mind, the rudiments of sin. The lower seam is like the believer's heart after entire sanctification has completed the work of purification; the pure love of God reigns alone without its opposites in any degree. There the graces of the Spirit exist in the soul without alloy, without mixture in simplicity. There is nothing contrary to them, and they exist in measure corresponding with the present capacity of the soul possessing them. Every buyer and seller is then excluded from the temple. No Canaanite remains in the land. We are ' delivered out of the hand of our enemies ', that we may ' serve God without fear in holiness and righteousness before Him all the days of our life '. The soul then enters upon the Sabbath rest of the love of God, and is filled with perfect peace.

CHAPTER VI

PURITY AND MATURITY

THERE are various degrees of impurity, but, strictly speaking, there are no degrees of purity. According to Webster, the word ' pure ' means : ' entire separation from all heterogeneous and extraneous matter, clear, free from mixture; as pure water, pure air, pure silver or gold '. The word in the New Testament which is most frequently translated ' pure ' occurs in some of its forms nearly seventy times. We may get at the idea the word was meant to convey by noting how the original is used. It is used of the body not smeared with paint or ointment, of an army rid of its sick and ineffective, of wheat when all the chaff has been winnowed away, of vines without excrescences, and of gold without alloy. The idea is that that which is pure consists of one thing; it is uncompounded, without mixture or adulteration, it has all that belongs to it and nothing else. Gold that is free from alloy, unmixed with any baser metal, we call pure gold; milk that contains all that belongs to milk, and nothing else, is pure milk; honey that is without wax is pure honey. In like manner a pure heart contains nothing adverse to God. Where there is mixture there cannot be purity. By purity of heart we mean that which is undefiled, untainted, free from evil stains, without earthly alloy. It is holiness unmixed with selfishness and pride, or any other polluting and debasing element. When this supernatural and divine work is wrought within us by the Holy Spirit, all the chaff, refuse, and dross are purged away and sifted out of the soul, and the precious residuum is the genuine, the true, the pure, and the good. Then the eye is single and the whole body is full of light. The graces exist in an unmixed state. Love exists without any germs of hatred, faith without any unbelief, humility without pride, meekness without any anger. 'Purity of heart is the removal of whatever God could not admit to His immediate presence, and fellowship with Himself; in other words, the abolition of sin itself.'

By maturity we mean all this, and much more. The error of confusing purity of heart with maturity of Christian character lies at the base of nearly all the objections made to instantaneous and entire sanctification. Identifying and confounding these have occasioned most of the difficulties we find among Christians in reference to this doctrine. The Scriptures always discriminate between purity of heart and the ripeness and fullness of Christian virtues. The one is a work wrought within us in a moment by the omnipotent power of the sanctifying Spirit, the other is a natural process involving culture and discipline. Purity has reference to kind or quality, but maturity has respect to degree or quantity. In 2 Corinthians vii. 1, the difference is clearly taught between holiness as a complete and immediate deliverance from all sin and the seemingly paradoxical doctrine of progressive holiness. Holiness is both a gift and a process, and as such it is both instantaneous and gradual, as this Scripture recognizes and explains: 'Having therefore these promises, dearly beloved, let us cleanse ourselves from all filthiness of the flesh and spirit; perfecting holiness in the fear of God.' By the 'flesh' we understand the lower animal nature which we have in common with the brute creation. The 'spirit' is the higher, nobler nature, designed to be the temple of God in man. The expression 'all filthiness of the flesh and spirit', embraces the whole of those evil propensities of our nature which would lead us to any kind of inordinate sensual indulgence, and all evil tempers, such as pride, envy, self-will, malice, uncharitableness, etc. It is that carnal and fleshly-mindedness of the heart which inheres to our fallen nature, the inward fountain, which we have already described, from which actual sins in the life have their rise. The phrase includes the whole of sin in man, the depraved nature in its entirety. Had the word 'all' been omitted, we should have been puzzled to know from how much sin we may be saved, and from how much we may not be saved. But this word covers the whole ground, the remedy extends to the last remains of sin.

As to when this deliverance may take place, the verb ' cleanse ' is in the aorist tense, which denotes that it is an instantaneous work. According to the best New Testament grammarians, we have no English tense exactly like the aorist in the Greek. It denotes a single momentary and decisive act, in opposition to a continuous and never-completed work. Hence says Dr. Beet : ' It is worthy of notice that in the New Testament we never read expressly and unmistakably of sanctification as a gradual process.' We grasp by faith the sin-consuming power which sweeps the heart clean at a stroke.

Cleansing is spoken of here as a human work, because it is by faith we appropriate the purifying power. On God's part all is done. The atonement is complete, the provisions ample. Christ's great work was restorative as well as atoning. Through the shedding of His blood He has procured for us cleansing as well as forgiveness. This is the teaching of the writer of the Epistle to the Hebrews : ' By the which will we are sanctified, through the offering of the body of Jesus once for all.' What is meant is that through His atoning work Christ has procured or purchased complete deliverance from sin for us exactly as He has made forgiveness possible to us. It is the will of God that we should be sanctified in the same way as we are justified ' through the offering of the body of Jesus once for all '. Provision is made for our sanctification as fully as for our justification. The human work in entire cleansing is to appropriate the salvation Christ has purchased and promised. The promises are the means and instruments of our cleansing. In order to cleanse a filthy garment, the fuller uses nitre and soap—both the fuller and soap are cleansers. So exactly is it with salvation, it is both a divine and human work. God provides the salvation, and we cleanse our soul by believing the promises.

I cannot wash my heart
But by believing Thee
And waiting for Thy blood to impart
The spotless purity.

But while the doctrine of instantaneous cleansing is undoubtedly taught by this text, the doctrine of progressive holiness is also taught. Being purged from all iniquity is one thing; a symmetrical, well-proportioned, and fully-developed Christian life is another. There can be no increase of purity, but there may be an eternal increase in love, and in all the fruits of the Spirit. After cleansing, our ceaseless prayerful effort must be to gain more knowledge, robuster virtue, deeper sanctity and every other form of spiritual excellence. This is what is implied by 'perfecting holiness in the fear of God'. The word 'perfecting' is defined in Baxter's Greek Testament Lexicon thus: 'to carry into practice, to realize', which means that the perfect inward cleansing instantaneously wrought by the Holy Spirit is to be constantly and progressively carried outward into all the acts of daily life. As knowledge increases and conscience is cultivated, there will be quickened sensibilities and more accurate perceptions of duty, which will lead to constant increase of moral beauty and all the fruits of righteousness, until we 'stand perfect and complete in all the will of God'.

It may not be generally known that the word 'health' and the word 'holy' come from the same root. Perfect health is the absence of disease, perfect holiness is the absence of sin. Christian purity brings finality to nothing but inbred sin. It is the soul restored to perfect health, but it is not perfect development. A babe may be perfectly healthy, but there is a vast difference between childhood and manhood. There are 'babes', 'young men', and 'men of full age', in a state of entire sanctification. Purity expels disease from the soul, maturity builds up the soul in vigour and beauty. The one is the field cleared of noxious weeds, the other is the ripe waving harvest. Purity is the best preparation for growth, but it is not the consummation of growth. A steady and constant growth in grace is the ideal in Christian life. But to secure this there must be a pure moral soil such as results from entire cleansing. ' The heart may be cleansed from all sin,' says Bishop Hamline, ' while our graces are immature, and entire cleansing is the best preparation for their unembarrassed and rapid growth.' We must seek a clean heart first, and look for maturity in the order of Divine appointment.

A friend of mine was once conversing with a good man and a leader in the Church on this important subject, when he said to him, ' I would just as soon believe that my son could go to school to-morrow morning without knowing a figure in arithmetic, and come home at night a complete mathematician, as I could believe that any man could in a day become a perfectly matured Christian.' My friend replied, ' You are confounding things that differ; I am speaking of one thing, and you of another '. ' Suppose ', he said, ' your son, with no knowledge of arithmetic, were to go to school to-morrow, and that he were put into simple addition, and that at the end of the month, and of the year and at the end of two or three years, he were in simple addition still, what would you say to that?' ' Why,' said he, ' I should say that there was something wrong in the boy, or in his teacher, or both.' ' Exactly,' replied my friend, ' that is just what I want you to see, that if we do not grow in grace, if we are always in a state of spiritual babyhood instead of advancing to manhood, it is because there is something wrong that needs removing.' That ' something ' is inbred or heart sin.

Purity is not the goal of Christian life, but rather a new starting-point on a higher plane. In conversion, all the graces of the Spirit are implanted within the soul, but they exist in germ only, they are not developed. So long as sin remains within us, not only are the graces of the Spirit within, but their opposites are there also, which are like weeds about the root of a plant impeding its growth. No grace of the Spirit can be helped in its development by the presence of its opposite. A little unbelief cannot help, but must hinder the growth of our faith, a little pride will have the same effect on our humility. To one who thought that we needed a little sin in our hearts to keep us humble, we ventured to suggest, ' Why not have a great deal, and be perfectly humble if there be reason in that?' Proclivities towards sin cannot help a soul into conformity to God. Just as a child, who has an organic disease, grows very slowly and unevenly, if at all, so a Christian who has not been entirely sanctified grows very irregularly. There must be perfect health before there can be real and vigorous growth. Sin in the heart makes us like a child that is sickly, or a tree with a worm at the root. Some hope by cultivating the graces of the Spirit to grow into purity, which is like a man cultivating the vegetables in his garden to grow the weed out from about the roots of the plants. Common sense says, ' Pluck up the weeds and give the plants a fair chance of growth and development.' This is the Divine method. God cleanses the heart from inbred sin, after which growth is more rapid and symmetrical; advancement in knowledge, the love of God, and every kind of grace become possible then, as never before. Purity of heart is not so much the enlargement and increase of the graces, as the plucking up of the weeds of inbred sin, which obstruct their growth. Maturity is the result of experience, trial, and conflict, it is a natural, gradual process of development, which requires time. But purity is by faith, and therefore a present and instantaneous experience. There may be preparations for it, and approaches to it, but there is a moment when the work is done.

Says Dr. Adam Clarke: ' We are to come to God for an instantaneous and complete purification from all sins, as for instantaneous pardon. In no part of the Scriptures are we directed to seek the remission of our sins *seriatim*—one now and another then, and so on. Neither a gradation pardon nor a gradation purification exists in the Bible. . . . For, as the work of renewing and cleansing the heart is the work of God, His Almighty power can perform it in a moment, in the twinkling of an eye.' *And it is this moment our duty* to love God with all our heart, and we cannot do this until He cleanse our hearts, consequently He is ready to do it this moment. . . . ' Believing now, we are pardoned now; believing now, we are cleansed from all sin now.'

But only as a complete deliverance from sin is holiness a present possibility. A mother is not content that her child should be in perfect health, she longs that it may grow to perfect maturity.' So deliverance from sin is but the stepping-stone, the vestibule and threshold of the higher life. Though a blessed and glorious state, yet when compared with the *breadth* and *length* and *depth* and *height* to which the soul may attain through the rich and abundant grace of God, it is not a really high state of spiritual attainment. None are so eager for spiritual advancement as those who are entirely sanctified. Like the racer who strains every nerve and muscle eager for the prize, they are always ' reaching forth unto those things which are before '. Their ideal is never reached, because the higher they climb the more the horizon enlarges to the view. The more God is known and loved, the more the soul ' follows hard after Him '. ' The path of the just is as the shining light, that shineth more and more unto the perfect day.' And even when the ' Perfect Day ' has come there will be continual progression in knowledge, love, and conformity to the image of the Lord Jesus, as the beauties of the God-man are unfolded before our enraptured vision.

CHAPTER VII

THE PRESENT TENSE OF CLEANSING

In meetings held for the promotion of holiness, we have often maintained that, so far as holiness is a deliverance from sin, the following points sum up the facts which cover the whole ground.

1. Does an infection of nature remain in regenerate persons?
2. If it does, may this infection of nature be entirely expelled from the soul?
3. If an infection of nature does remain in regenerate persons, and this may be entirely expelled, when may the deliverance take place?

Most Christians assent readily enough to the first two of these propositions, but there is considerable difference of opinion as to the third, when this salvation may be obtained. Some say at death, others after a long period of growth; but we believe it may be a present and instantaneous experience. We do not mean instantaneous in the same sense as a flash of lightning, or an explosion of gunpowder, but in the sense in which death is instantaneous. ' A man be a long time dying, but there is a moment when he dies.'

There is no denial that sin must be wholly destroyed in us before we can be meet for the inheritance of the saints. All believe that entire sanctification is necessary to admission to heaven, but not a few have discrowned Christ as the Saviour, and are waiting for death to do what they think he cannot, or will not, do. Our Bibles teach us concerning the time, the means, and the agent of sanctification, but nowhere is it taught that death is any of these. We do read that ' the last enemy to be destroyed is death ', but if death brings deliverance from sin he can hardly be described as an ' enemy '. If this were true, instead of being 'the last enemy' he would be the last friend, and the best friend, too. What is death? It is the separation of the soul from the body. But the mere separation of the soul from the body will not destroy sin in the soul, and only the soul can be the seat of sin.

It is to be feared that those who have no expectation of deliverance from sin until death comes to the help of Jesus have got hold of a relic of Gnosticism—a heresy which was early introduced into Christianity as a corrupting element. The Gnostics taught that in all matter was evil—ineradicable evil. Because our bodies are composed of matter, they believed there was evil in the body; and because the spirit dwells in such a body, it is tainted, and must be till this 'mortal puts on immortality'. But the idea of sin in the body is totally unscriptural, as it is palpably absurd. No body, or matter of any kind, can be sinful; spirits alone are capable of sin. To teach that our spirits will be cleansed from sin after death is to accept the Papal doctrine of purgatory. The soul must be purified, therefore, in the moment of death or before; and we have already shown that the mere separation of the soul from the body will not effect this change. When, then, will this cleansing take place? Before death necessarily. And if it is Christ who saves from sin, why not now? With Him there is no such thing as time. Centuries, years, months, weeks, days, are nothing to God. 'One day is with the Lord as a thousand years, and a thousand years as one day.' If we have fulfilled the conditions, God is as able and willing to save from all sin now, as He will be a moment before death.

As we obtained pardon by simple faith, so we must obtain purity. We are no more able to work out the latter in our hearts than the former. Sin is not a thing to be grown out of, but something to be cleansed away. 'Every branch in Me that beareth fruit He purgeth it.' The branch that is covered with blight does not grow out of the blight. The branch that has too much wood, and needs pruning, does not secure the pruning by growth. It is pruned in order that the hindering thing may be removed and growth promoted. Purity is something removed, growth is something added. Growth in grace is a natural process, the enlargement or development of some living force; holiness is the gift of God, a supernatural work wrought in the soul by the Holy Ghost. The soul can no more grow pure than the growth of a plant can kill or destroy the worm at its root. Purity and growth are as distinct in their offices as the work of two men on a building —one is removing the rubbish, the other is enlarging and beautifying the structure. In growth we are active and co-operative, but in entire cleansing the soul is passive, it is something experienced, the same as regeneration. It is a special miracle of grace—the power of God invoked by faith, for this particular end, and consequently instantaneously received.

But holiness is some immutable state which we attain by a desperate venture of faith once for all; it is rather a condition of soul which requires for its maintenance the continual observance of the conditions by which we enter into it.

'Do you teach the possibility of an absolute death of sin?' asked an undergraduate during a mission which I held in Oxford some years ago. 'No,' was my reply, 'we teach the possibility of a conditional death of sin.' 'What is the difference, may I ask, between a conditional death of sin and an absolute death?' he further inquired. My answer was as follows :—' Suppose there were no windows in this building and it were full of darkness, how are we to get rid of the darkness? A strong light is brought in, and when the light fills the building the darkness is excluded. But the darkness is only excluded so long as the light remains. If we remove the light, the darkness returns. Let the darkness represent sin, and the light holiness. What the light is to the dark room the Holy Spirit is to the heart of the believer. When He fills the heart with the light of His own indwelling presence all sin is excluded, but that condition is only maintained so long as the Holy Spirit continues fully to possess the heart. By one act the room becomes instantly lighted, but if it be continued in a state of illumination the presence of the light must be continued. So to retain the Holy Spirit's presence within us, and the purity which the radiating power of His own most blessed presence produces, requires a continual walking in the light, and the continual acting of the same faith by which we first received it.'

Holiness is both a *crisis* and a *process*. As Bishop Moule would say,' It is a crisis with a view to a process '. A crisis is undoubtedly reached when, after full surrender of all we have, and are, to the Lord Jesus, we venture out upon the promise with an appropriating act, ' the blood of Jesus Christ His Son cleanseth "*me, even me*", from all sin '. When we believe this, the Holy Spirit comes to our hearts in sanctifying power, excluding all the evil, and filling us with Divine love, just as He came to our hearts in re-generating power when we believed for forgiveness and were adopted into the family of God. The heart is only cleansed from all sin by the Holy Spirit taking full possession of it, and it is only kept clean by His remaining in full possession. We teach, therefore, not a *state of purity,* but a *maintained condition of purity,* a moment-by-moment salvation consequent upon a moment-by-moment obedience and trust. ' The blood of Jesus Christ cleanseth us from all sin ' *all the time* by cleansing us every *now.*

Blessed word ' *cleanseth* '—present progressive tense—it goes on cleansing. Does it not teach, as Miss Havergal puts it, ' a continual present, always a present tense, not a present which the next moment becomes a past, not a coming to be cleansed in the fountain only, but a remaining in the fountain ' ? It means ever-present provision for ever-present need ; Christ is always a present Saviour. We are kept clean like the eyes of a miner who is working all day amid the flying coal-dust. When he emerges into daylight his face is grimy enough, but his eyes are clear and lustrous, because the fountain of tears in the lachrymal gland is ever pouring its gentle tides over the eyes, cleansing away each speck of dust as it alights. Our spirits need a similiar cleansing, and this is what our blessed Lord does for us, as we believe moment by moment 'that the blood cleanseth '.

The habit of faith must be acquired. Faith in the spiritual world has been compared to breathing in the physical. We breathe this moment and receive the oxygen into our lungs, it purifies the blood which goes coursing through the system, carrying life and nutriment to all the tissues; but when another moment comes we must breathe again, another moment again, and so on. Life is made up of successive acts of breathing. We breathe moment by moment, and live moment by moment. If we cease to breathe, we cease to live. In like manner, we trust the blood of Jesus for cleansing this moment, and it cleanseth from all sin; another moment comes, and we trust again, and another moment yet again, and so on. We are thus kept clean exactly as we are made clean, through a constant succession of acts of faith in the cleansing blood. But this habit of faith requires time to establish. Every habit grows out of a succession of little acts. The faith that cleanses our hearts from sin requires a definite effort at first, but repeated moment by moment it becomes spontaneous, and by and by, natural as breathing. The habit becomes a necessity and easier as it grows.

But only as we walk in the light does the blood of Jesus cleanse from all sin. Should there be a moment's hesitation about yielding, obeying, or trusting, communion with God will be broken, and darkness and sin will return. We must not only maintain a perpetual attitude of self-surrender and abandonment to the will of God, but our consecration must keep pace with the ever-widening circle of illumination. Most believers over whom Satan gets an advantage are either disobedient to one of God's written commands or to the inward promptings of the Holy Spirit. The blood, however, never loses its virtue, and whenever, in our walk in the light, we are sensible of the least soil of evil, we may wash again and be clean.

As already explained, holiness expresses that state of

soundness in the spiritual part of man which corresponds to health in the physical part of man; but our souls, like our bodies, are liable to disease, though at present they may be in perfect health. Just as to maintain bodily health we must observe the laws of health, so to maintain spiritual health, we must moment by moment trust and obey.

CHAPTER VIII

A GOD-POSSESSED SOUL

IN previous chapters we have described holiness as that
state of grace in which all sin is excluded from the heart,
but there is always a positive as well as a negative aspect
of spiritual life. This is true both of the new birth and
entire sanctification. In conversion the negative aspect is
pardon, the positive is regeneration, the impartation of
the life of God to the soul. There are no degrees of
pardon: it is full, perfect, and complete; but on the
positive side perpetual increase is the order: there is ' life ',
and ' more abundant life '. In like manner, while the
negative aspect of holiness is the purging of the heart
from all that is carnal—and this is a full, complete and
entire work, without degrees and gradualism—there is also
a positive aspect of holiness which is never separate from
the negative; the one always implies the other. This
positive blessing is the complete filling of the soul with the
life of God. Justification is our coming to Christ; sanctification is Christ coming to us. Entire sanctification is to be
entirely possessed by Christ—so filled with His life that
sin and Satan are cast out. We must not simply possess
life, but the life must possess us. Sin flies before the Divine
presence as darkness flies before the light. All would be
darkness but for the presence of the light; and all would
be sin within us but for the presence of the life.

> What Thou fillest, Lord, is pure,
> What Thou keepest can endure ;
> But Thy temple, void of Thee,
> Foul, not only frail, must be.

Some teach that the condition on which God dwells in
the soul is the soul's purifying itself to receive Him; but we
cannot cleanse our hearts so as to bring Christ into them;
we must let Him come and cleanse them by the process of
His coming, and so fit them for His own indwelling. It is

the work of the great Master Himself to thoroughly purge His floor, and until He does it, it must remain defiled. But His coming, which ' is like a refiner's fire, and like fuller's soap ', burns up the filthiness, purges away the dross, and makes the heart capable of His own more entire indwelling.

We are in the habit of saying that Christ saves us by His death on the cross. In an important sense this is true, but it is not the whole truth. We need Christ *in* us as much as we need His death *for* us. By dependence upon that one great past act of Christ when He died on the cross we have forgiveness, but to be cleansed from indwelling sin and to live the overcoming life we must have Christ Himself dwelling within us as a present living Saviour. It is only as we receive Him into our hearts, and in proportion as we submit to His possession and control, that the life of holiness is in any sense possible. But He offers to come to us in His person, and to become to each and all an indwelling life, which will literally reproduce in us His own purity, and enable us to live among men as He lived.

Christ speaks of Himself as abiding in His people, and of His life flowing through them as the life of the vine flows through the branches. As at the Transfiguration, where, through the thin veil of His humanity, His divinity burst forth, so is the life of holiness. It is simply the outshining of the Divine life which is within us. ' Sanctity,' says an old writer, ' is nothing else than the life of Jesus Christ in man, whom it transforms, so to speak, by anticipation, making him to appear, even here below, in some measure what he shall be when the Lord shall come in glory.' If Christ be in full possession of our hearts, it will not be long before we are doing in our poor way some of the beautiful things He would do if He were here Himself in bodily form. That He may reproduce His own life in ours is the great purpose of His indwelling, and this is the secret of holy living.

There is none holy but the Lord, and He will come and take up His abode in the centre of our being, and thence purify the whole house through and through by the radiating power of His own blessed presence. As to the woman of Samaria, who asked that she might drink of the living water, the Saviour promised that the *well* should be in her; so to us, not His gifts but *Himself* will He give. If we get the Bridegroom, we shall get His possessions. How superior in permanency is the Giver over the gift! The latter may be evanescent, but the former comes to abide. 'We will come,' Christ said, including the Father with Himself, 'and make our abode with him.' This is something which the Old Testament saints never knew. God was *with* Abraham, Moses and Elijah; but God now dwells *within* the humblest of His saints who sincerely receive Him. This is the mystery hid from ages and generations: 'Christ in you, the hope of glory.' This is 'the wisdom of God in a mystery, even the wisdom which none of the princes of this world knew'. 'Christ made unto us of God, wisdom, even righteousness, sanctification, and redemption.' This is the great provision of the Gospel, a living personal Saviour, Christ our life.

Heathen writers speak of virtue, which means to them the repression of evil; but of holiness—the outshining of Divine life—they know nothing. Christianity is the only religion in the world which teaches that God dwells within men, as certainly as of old the Shekinah dwelt in the most holy place. In His earthly life, Christ said that the Father dwelt in Him so really that the words He spoke and the works He did were not His own, but His Father's. And He desires to be in us as His Father was in Him, so thinking in our thoughts, and willing in our will, and working in our actions, that we may be the channels through which He, hidden within, may pour Himself forth upon men, and that we may repeat in some small measure the life of Jesus on the earth. This is our all-sufficiency for every situation, and trial, and difficulty. In Him are all the treasures of wisdom, knowledge and power, and when He comes to abide with us, it is like a beggar having a prince to come to live with him. He places all His

resources at our disposal, and bids us draw upon Him.
'According to the riches of His glory' is the measure of
His supply. A king gives like a king, a God works like a
God. He wants to do in us and through us something
worthy of Himself. 'I cannot,' to the call of duty is a
libel on the lips of the man who calls himself a Christian.
If you cannot, Christ can, and He is in you to meet every
need as it arises. 'He is able to make all grace to abound
towards us, so that we have a sufficiency for all emergencies,
and can abound in every good work.' We have no space
to elaborate the thought, but as the Holy Spirit unfolds
to us the wealth hidden within us now that Christ has come
to our hearts, we shall be able to say, with ever-increasing
confidence, 'I can do all things in Him that strengtheneth
me' (Phil. iv. 13, R.V.).

This aspect of truth makes Christ prominent, and shows
what He is to us as contrasted with some attainment which
might call attention to ourselves. An illustration will
explain what I mean. Suppose I held in my hand a piece
of iron. We will imagine that it can speak. It says, I am
hard, I am cold, I am black. But we put the iron into the
fire. The fire comes into it, and a wonderful transformation
follows; it has not ceased to be iron, but the blackness is
gone, and the coldness is gone, and the hardness is gone.
It has entered into a new experience. If that iron could
speak it would not glory in itself, but in the fire that keeps
it a bright and glowing mass. Withdraw the fire from it,
and the coldness, the hardness and the blackness begin at
once to return. The fire makes the difference. So is it
with the believer. Without Christ 'we are carnal, and sold
unto sin', like the iron, hard, cold and black; but when
Christ comes to possess us we are filled with light, love and
power. This transformation is more wonderful than the
effect of the fire upon the iron. We enter upon a new
experience, not only of emancipation from sin, but of
peace, and joy and victory. But do we glory in something
we have attained? We have attained nothing, Christ's
indwelling makes the difference. The experience can have

4

no existence apart from Christ Himself, so we glory in Him.

It is impossible to emphasize too strongly that Christ must do all in us, just as He has already done all for us. Not that He and we are to do the work between us. Salvation is of God from beginning to end. Well might we despair if the life of holiness depended upon human strength or resources, but all the difficulties vanish when God undertakes the work. The whole ground is covered by provision and promise. Because Christ died we have life, because His life is in us we are dead to sin. It is not simply that Christ took our death, we must take His life. We receive Christ into our hearts by faith, and we keep Him there by a faith which produces holiness.

But some have Christ who are not entirely possessed by Christ. Instead of the unbroken blessedness which accompanies the perpetual realization of Christ's continuous abiding, so far as their consciousness is concerned, His visits are short and far between, and their fellowship broken and interrupted. The reason is they have never consecrated themselves fully to Christ. It is of no use for such to pray for more of God, God wants more of them. When the self-life expires, Christ will possess us fully for Himself as naturally as air rushes into a vacuum. We create the vacuum by dethroning our idols. Nearly all the delay, difficulty and danger lies at this point, unwillingness to fully surrender to Christ and to have no will of our own. Self can assert itself just as effectually in a little as in a great thing. It may be some very trifling thing that is exempted from the dominion of Christ—some preference, some indulgence, some humiliating duty, some association to be broken, or some adornment to be discarded, but never until self is crucified can we learn the full meaning of being Christ-possessed.

We must have empty hands to grasp a whole Christ. St. Paul could never have said, 'I am crucified with Christ; it is no longer I that live, but Christ liveth in me' (Alford), had self been still alive disputing with Christ the throne of the soul. Self had been nailed to the cross, and

Christ had taken the supreme place in his soul. Luther testifies to a very similiar experience. ' If any person knocks at the door of my heart and asks who lives here, I shall answer, Not Martin Luther, *he died some time ago;* Jesus Christ lives here.' Just as where the self-seeking Jacob died the prevailing Israel was begotten, so from the ashes of our self-life shall come the prevailing life. It is only when the last entrenchment of self-will has been surrendered that there can be a complete resurrection unto life. But when we are ready to say, ' There is nothing that would dishonour Christ that I will not forsake, nothing that would bring glory to Him which I will not render or perform; I will give myself and all I have into His hands for time and for eternity; I will follow Christ whithersoever He goes ', Christ will not be long in taking full possession. With all His blessings He will enter our hearts, purging us from our evil, and so revealing Himself to our inner consciousness, that henceforth, in an unbroken line of deep calm receptiveness, we may possess, and know that we possess, an indwelling Saviour.

Do any of my readers say what those two on the way to Emmaus said to the Master, ' Abide with us, abide with us ' ? His answer *is* already given, ' This is My rest for ever, here will I dwell, for I have desired it, even in this poor heart of thine'.

CHAPTER IX

PERFECT LOVE

In the New Testament there are two words for love. One is *philos*, which is the word used to express natural human affection. This exists in greater or less degree throughout the entire animal kingdom, including all natural affections of human nature apart from Divine grace. The other word, *agape*, is invariably used to express a Divine affection, imparted to the soul by the Holy Ghost. Natural love existed within us before we were regenerated, as it exists in human nature generally; but of Divine love we had none until we were born into the kingdom of God. The love of God was then ' shed abroad in our hearts ', and by this alone can we claim the title of children of God, as partakers of His nature. ' The love of God here means not our love to God, nor exactly the sense of God's love to us, but *God's love itself for us.*' ' Behold what manner of love the Father has bestowed upon us,' not manifested or demonstrated, but *bestowed,* imparted, given to us as a gift. What a wonderful truth this is, that God's love *for* us shall be *in* us, and become our love to others. Was this not what our Lord asked for when He prayed, ' that the love wherewith Thou hast loved Me may be in them, and I in them ' ? The truth declared is that God gives us His love to love with; He has made His love our property, absolutely given it to us, so that it is now ours. Who can tell all that this means? Inspiration itself can only find relief in adoring gratitude. ' Behold what manner of love.'

Perhaps we shall now better understand the new commandment to love ' as I have loved you '. · On Calvary we see love stronger than death. There we learn what love really is, and what it can do. When that same love drives our chariot wheels, we shall be ready to do as He did. It is where sacrifice begins that the proof of love begins. We must not offer, either to God or man, what costs nothing.

The noblest thing in God's world is a lavished life. Carnal selfish men cannot understand the service and sacrifice of those

> Who spend their lives for others,
> With no ends of their own.

But when our love is in *kind* like His, we cannot help doing it. Our '*must*' then is like the '*must*' of God. God must give His love, whether souls accept it or not. Let the love of Christ, the most sublime of all motives, and the glory of Christ, the most sublime of all ends, become the ruling principle of action, and who can help living magnanimously for man and for God?

More of Christ's love in our hearts means always increased sympathy with His dominant passion, the salvation of the lost. There is a grave mistake somewhere when a person imagines that he has mounted up to the plane of the 'high life', and feels no quickened impulse towards those who are perishing in their sins around him. Zeal in soul-winning is only love on fire. Give us more of the hidden fire, and all the rest will follow.

In serving the poor, the suffering, and the lost, we serve Him, and nothing is counted too good for Him by those who are filled with His sanctifying love. We prove our love to Christ by what we do for our fellow-creatures. Love cannot treat its Lord meanly. She will not give Him the remnant, the drift, and the dregs of life. Giving of our surplus is no proof of love at all. She always offers the most that is possible, and the best. The one motive that has the power to lift us out of self, and to exalt life to its highest and loftiest phase, is a heart brimful of love to Christ. 'For Christ's sake.' These three little words are the touchstone of love.

Jeremy Taylor represents Ivo as going on an embassy to St. Louis, and meeting a strange woman, who had fire in one hand and water in the other. He asked what these strange symbols meant, and she replied : 'With fire I shall burn up heaven, and with water quench the flames of hell, that men may serve God without incentives, either of hope or fear, for His own sake.' This is what Perfect Love does. If there were no heaven, and if there were no hell, hearts filled with the love of God would serve Him just the same. Love service is the spontaneous, glad offering of a grateful heart, like that of the woman who broke the box of ointment and poured it on the feet of Christ. It is not clearer views of our duty to God that will win us over to new obedience; but as the love of Jesus floods our souls, a deeper, fuller, and ever augumenting stream, the life of duty becomes transformed into a life of liberty and delight.

'Perfect love casteth out fear.' The two words 'love' and 'fear', placed in contrast in this Scripture, represent the two different motives that may actuate us in Christian service. Some serve from love, as Jacob did in the pastures of Laban; and some from fear, like the Hebrews in the brickfields of Egypt. Mrs. Pearsall Smith puts the difference well; it is simply the difference between 'may I' and 'must I', between enjoyment and endurance. In law service we do our duty, but too often as the unwilling schoolboy creeps off to school; but in love service the will is won, and we do our work not like the slave under the lash, but with eagerness and joy.

How sluggishly the men in yonder workshop are using their tools; how they weary for the hour of dismissal to strike! But after they have rushed away home, you might have seen one youth remaining, singing at his work; and when you ask the reason, he sweetly said. 'Those others are hirelings, paid by the hour, but I have an interest in the business; it is my father's business, and a loving father he has been to me.' Alas! how many Christians forget that they are sons, and work for wages as hirelings do. Perhaps in most Christians the two motives exist together, the pure gold of love is mingled with the dross of fear in service; but when our love is 'made perfect', our will elects God's will with unspeakable gladness. We shall keep the law then, not from dread of its penalties, but from love for the law itself, and the Lawgiver. Filled with Divine love, we love what God loves, and in this condition the will of God is no longer as a yoke upon the neck; Christ's service is perfect freedom. Faber sings:

> He hath breathed into my heart
> A special love of Thee,
> A love to lose my will in His,
> And by the loss be free.

This is not freedom from law; that would be licence. Nor is it being under law; that would be bondage. It is being *inlawed,* God putting the law into our love, so that we keep it from our very love of it, by a glad assent as naturally as water runs down-hill. Before we reach this experience we are often like a man carrying a burden up-hill, but when we reach it the burden and the hill suddenly disappear, and we can joyfully appropriate the words of the Son of God, and say, ' I delight to do Thy will, O my God; yea, Thy law is within my heart '.

The old Covenant was an outside, coercive force, a law written in stone. The new Covenant is written in the heart, rectifying and inspiring all the springs of action. God fulfils the promise of the new Covenant, ' I will put My law into your hearts ', when His love is so fully shed abroad in the heart of the believer as to effect a complete release from the fear of the law as a motive to obedience.

Never, until the love of God becomes the all-absorbing, all-controlling, dominating principle of life, can we understand the seeming contradiction in Psalm cxvi. 16, ' O Lord, truly I am Thy servant; I am Thy servant, and the son of Thine handmaid : *Thou hast loosed my bonds* '. But when every faculty is energized, every capacity filled, and the whole nature pervaded with this transcendent gift, the bondage, the irksomeness, the subtle legalism which more or less characterize the service of incipient believers, are entirely removed. The yoke of Christ no longer chafes, the last trace of servile feeling is gone, and the will of God becomes our free, spontaneous, delightful choice. We can sing then, not as mere poetic fancy, but as a glorious experimental reality—

I worship Thee, sweet will of God,
    And all Thy ways adore ;
And every day I live, I seem
    To love Thee more and more.

But do you ask, ' How am I to enter into this blessed experience? We brace our wills to secure it. We try to copy those who have it. We lay down rules about it. We watch, we pray; but these things do not bring the fullness of love into our souls.' Love is never produced by straining and struggling, or by any direct action of the soul upon itself. ' A man in a boat cannot move it by pressing it from within.' Love is an effect, and here is the cause. We receive love when we receive God. If we would have love we must seek Him. God is love, and love is God. More love means more of God. Perfect love means that we have opened all the avenues of our being, and that He has come and taken possession of every chamber. Some writer has said, ' Take love from an angel and you have a devil, take love from a man and you have a brute, take love from God and there is nothing left '. When Sir James Mackintosh was dying, a friend saw his lips move, and when the ear was put down it caught the whisper, ' God— Love—the very same '. Yes, love is the only word convertible with God. It is not His mere name, but His nature —His being—Himself. When He comes to the heart, He comes not empty-handed. He brings His love with Him, and that, consciously received, produces a corresponding and answering love in our hearts to Him. Says Lange, ' When God's love to us comes to be in us, it is like the virtue which the loadstone gives to the needle, inclining it to move towards the pole.' There is no need to ask whether the Perfect Love of which St. John speaks means Christ's love to us, or our love to Christ. It is both. The recognition of His love, and the response of ours, are the result of His entering and abiding in the heart. ' He that has made his home in love has his home in God, and God has His home in him.'

CHAPTER X

EVANGELICAL PERFECTION

THE Scriptural terms 'holiness', 'perfect love', 'perfection', may be used synonymously, because they all point to the same state of grace. John Fletcher says: 'We frequently use, as St. John, the phrase "perfect love" instead of perfection; understanding by it the pure love of God shed abroad in the hearts of established believers by the Holy Ghost, which is abundantly given unto them under the fullness of the Christian dispensation.' But while these terms may be used indiscriminately in speaking of full salvation, each one indicates some essential characteristic and emphasizes some different aspect of the truth. Perfect love is expressive of the spirit and temper, or the moral atmosphere in which the entirely sanctified Christian lives. Perfection signifies that spiritual completeness or wholeness into which the soul enters when the last inward foe is conquered, and the last distracting force harmonized with the mighty love of Christ, every crevice of the nature filled with love, and every energy employed in the delightful service of our adorable Saviour. This implies not only complete deliverance from all spiritual pollution, but the possession of the unmixed graces of faith, humility, resignation, patience, meekness, self-denial, and all other graces of the Spirit.

No word has been the occasion of so much stumbling and controversy among Christians as this word 'perfect'. But the term is a spiritual one and is used more frequently in the Bible than any other single term to set forth Christian experience. It occurs one hundred and thirty-eight times in the Scriptures, and in more than fifty of these instances it refers to human character under the operation of grace. Early in Divine revelation, we find Jehovah saying to Abraham, 'Walk before Me, and be thou perfect', and to Moses, 'Thou shalt be perfect with the Lord'. Forty-five times the Israelites are commanded to bring sacrifices

without blemish, and every time the word should have been
translated perfect. By such impressive symbols, God would
teach that the heart of the offerer must be perfect before
Him. Opening the New Testament, we find the word
' perfect ' dropping from the lips of Christ, and from the
pen of St. Paul, seventeen times as descriptive of fitness
for the kingdom of God; while the cognate noun *perfection*
is twice used, and the verb *to perfect* fourteen times.
Instead of finding fault with a word which the Spirit of
inspiration sees fit to use with such persistency from the
Book of Genesis to the Epistles of St. John, should we not
rather endeavour to arrive at its true Scriptural meaning?

That the term needs to be guarded against fanaticism
and superstition we do not deny. We are not to regard
it in an absolute sense, nor without due discrimination.
Absolute perfection, which is the combination of all conceivable excellences in the highest degree, belongs only to
God, and to that perfection no mortal or seraph can ever
attain. Between the highest degree of human perfection
and the perfection of God, there must ever be all the
difference which there is between the finite and the infinite.

Holy as Thou, O Lord, is none.

Nor can we in this present life attain the perfection of
the celestial world. The love of a glorified saint will burn
with an intensity, and his service be performed with a
precision and rectitude impossible on earth. In the third
chapter of the Epistle to the Philippians, St. Paul seems
to breathe hot and cold with the same breath to those who
do not read carefully. First, he declares that he is not
perfect (Phil. iii. 12), and then immediately afterwards
speaks of himself and others as being perfect (Phil. iii. 15).
But there is really no contradiction, because two different
kinds of perfection are spoken of. He was referring to the
perfection of the glorified state when he said, ' Not as
though I had already attained, either were already perfect '.
Bengel says, ' Crowned with a garland of victory, his course
completed '. This is evident from the context. ' I count

all things, but loss, if by any means I might attain unto
the resurrection of the dead.' None who examine the
chapter closely and without prejudice will dispute that the
apostle speaks here of a perfection which will follow the
resurrection of the righteous dead. To this St. Paul
aspired : ' Reaching forth unto those things which are
before, I press toward the mark for the prize of the high
calling of God in Christ Jesus.' Not until then will our
brightest ideals of perfection be realized. But the words,
' Let us therefore, as many as be perfect, be thus minded ',
obviously refer to a perfection which, in another and
intelligible sense, is possible in this life, and to which he
had already attained.

We must distinguish also between evangelical perfection,
which we believe to be a present possibility, and the
perfection of full and completed growth. Often in the
New Testament the word perfect is used in reference to
those who are no longer babes but ' fathers ' in Christ. The
graces of the new life have attained a certain ripeness and
maturity, so that there is a strong and well-developed manhood. To attain this perfection requires time. It is the
result of sedulous cultivation of the heart, patient study of
God's Word, earnest attention to all means of grace, and
close walking with God. Unto this perfection of degree,
of development, of full growth, of final attainment, the
exhortation is always, ' Let us go on '. There is no finality,
no point beyond which we may not move. Such perfection
may be approximated but never reached; ' it is an eternal
approximation towards an unrealizable ideal '. ' That your
love may abound yet more and more,' will always be an
appropriate prayer. There is no *ne plus ultra* in Christian
experience.

The Greeks had two words which we translate ' perfect '.
One meant to make fully ready, the other meant to complete or finish. The former applies to a person or thing
which is quite fitted and thoroughly furnished for its
purpose : ' Made perfect in every good work to do His
will.' The second is used to express perfection in the sense

of completeness, which results from growth and experience :
' Till we are come in the unity of the faith, and of the
knowledge of the Son of God unto a *perfect* man, unto
the measure of the stature of the fullness of Christ.'

By evangelical perfection we mean perfection in the first
of these uses of the word. Its principal ideas are adaption
and endowment. Those who are Christianly perfect are
fully fitted and equipped for the service of God and the
Church in one department or another, as is most suitable
to the gifts and graces of each individual. (2 Tim. iii. 17 ;
Eph. iv. 11, 12 ; Heb. xiii. 20, 21.) One form of the word
is used by Matthew and Mark when they state that Jesus
found the sons of Zebedee *mending* or perfecting their
nets, which suggests that in order to be fully qualified for
Christian service, all the rents which sin has made in our
spiritual nature must be repaired. There must be spiritual
wholeness, the powers of the soul must no longer be reduced
in tone or hindered in their development by remaining evil.
Whatever is contrary to love must be cleansed away, and
all the graces of the Spirit being present, the believer is
then fully filled or equipped for service and progress. Many
Christians are not much used of God because they are not
thus furnished or adjusted for the activities and ministra-
tions of spiritual life. A man might as well try to work
or to run with a dislocated limb as a Christian expect to
be able to do best work or make rapid progress without
this preliminary perfecting. Perfection, in the sense of
mending or repairing, is only and always used with a
view to perfect action. Christianity knows nothing of a
holiness that does not manifest itself in outward obedience
to God and active service to man.

We subscribe to every word of John Fletcher's definition
of a Christian perfection : ' The pure love of God shed
abroad in the heart by the Holy Ghost given unto us, to
cleanse us and keep us clean from all filthiness of flesh and
spirit, and to enable us to fulfil the law of Christ, according
to the talents we are entrusted with, and the circumstances
in which we are placed in the world.'

Richard Hooker, in speaking of perfection, says: 'We count those things perfect which want nothing for the end whereunto they were instituted.' In other words, if a thing answers the end for which it was designed, it is perfect. A weighing-machine constructed to weigh a hundredweight is perfect if it weighs a hundredweight exactly. Because such a machine will not weigh a ton, do we find fault with it, and say it is not perfect? To do so would be very unjust, because the maker only designed it to weigh a hundredweight. In like manner we may be perfect in the sense of answering the end for which God made us, but for any other purpose far removed from perfection. Many who object to Christian perfection want the machine to weigh more than God intended. In many respects we may be very imperfect, but if we love God with all the capacity we actually possess, we are Christianly perfect according to the Scriptures. 'Herein is our love made perfect, that we may have boldness in the day of judgement.' We are no more expected to be perfect as God is, or as the angels are, or as Adam was, than a machine constructed to weigh a hundredweight is expected to be able to weigh a ton.

Evangelical perfection embraces two things:—

(1) A perfection of love proportioned to the Powers of each individual;

(2) A steady progress in love harmonizing with our circumstances and our increasing capacity and ability.

'Thou shalt love the Lord thy God with all thy heart, and with all thy soul, and with all thy mind, and with all thy strength.' There is no statute in the Bible which sets up or requires any other standard. 'Love is the fulfilling of the law.' God requires nothing more; He could demand nothing less. Love is to be complete to the extent of the present capacity of the person possessing it. We are not required to love God with an archangel's powers, nor with the strength of a Rutherford, a Fletcher, or a Bramwell.

With all thy heart, is the command. Our love-power may be very limited, but so long as it is fully employed in loving God, we fulfil the Divine requirement just the same as those who have the larger capacities. A thimble may be as full as a bucket. To love God with more than all our heart—beyond our power or capacity—would be impossible; and to love Him less than to the full measure of our power to love, would be short of His requirement. ' He that does as well as he can, does well : angels can do no better, and God requires no more.'

But we are asked, ' How can that which is perfect admit of increase? ' A circle of twenty-four inches diameter is a perfect circle, and so is one of twelve inches in diameter. Both are perfect circles, but one is larger than the other. A perfect child, a perfect lamb, a perfect sapling, are susceptible of growth, so always the perfect Christian will be. It is true he cannot love God with more than all his heart—beyond his power or capacity—that would be an absurdity; but the capacities of the soul are expansive and progressive, and love in measure can and will increase, as capacity increases, to an unlimited extent. Love-power develops by its exercise just as an intellectual power does. A vessel cannot be more than full, but we may have a larger vessel. It is because ours may be an ever-expanding capacity that an ever-increasing love is possible.

Some teach that Christian perfection may be approximated, but never reached—a sort of constant advance towards a point we can never gain. But we are not commanded simply to aspire after it,

WE ARE REQUIRED TO POSSESS IT.

And the experience is to be a present one. Grammarians tell us that all commands are in the present tense. As Dr. Steele puts it, ' if they cover the future they include the indivisible now.' We all understand the command, ' Repent ye ! ' to mean repent just now, because the future is all uncertain. And exactly in like manner ' Be ye holy ' requires present holiness. ' Be ye perfect ' enjoins perfection to-day. 'Thou shalt love the Lord thy God with all thy heart,' means nothing at all if it does not mean that our love is to be made perfect now.

Let no person stagger at this immediateness. God always gives power to comply with His requirements. Duties are privileges, and all commands are equivalent to promises. The man with the withered hand in the synagogue knew well enough that the command, 'Stretch forth thine hand', meant that Christ would give ability to obey. And just as sure may we be that the command to love God now with a perfect love, implies that He will give us power to do what He requires us to do. To maintain otherwise is to charge God with mocking us with a command we are utterly unable to perform. What God requires *now* must be possible *now;* and if we will but claim as a present privilege what He reveals as a present duty, we shall immediately prove that 'the word is very nigh unto thee, in thy mouth, and in thy heart, that thou mayest do it!' And what is this word of promise, but 'the Lord thy God will circumcise thine heart, and the heart of thy seed, to love the Lord thy God with all thine heart, and with all thy soul, that thou mayest live'? (Deut. xxx. 6 and 14.)

CHAPTER XI

THE FULLNESS OF THE SPIRIT

At the Council of Jerusalem (Acts xv. 8, 9) Peter, in giving an account of his visit to Cornelius, and the work of God upon the hearts of those assembled, said : ' And God, who knoweth the hearts, bare them witness, giving them the Holy Ghost, even as He did to us; and put no difference between us and them, purifying their hearts by faith.'

Two facts are here stated :—

1. That the same fullness of the Spirit which the apostles received at Pentecost was imparted to Cornelius and his household.

2. That the work wrought was the purifying of their hearts by faith.

The conclusion is inevitable that the baptism of the Holy Ghost includes entire cleansing from sin, or, in other words, that the fullness of the Spirit is a synonym for entire sanctification. Since there are but two forces which can sway the soul, the flesh and the Spirit, to be completely filled with either is to exclude the other. All inward renewal is the result of the Holy Spirit's operation; He is the indispensable agent in the production of spiritual life, both in its beginnings and in its fullness. Theologians speak of God, the Father, as the *originating cause* of salvation; of Christ as the *procuring cause*; of the Holy Spirit as the ' *executive of the Godhead* '. This latter phrase, coined by Dr. Hodge, of America, very aptly describes the work of the Third Person in the Trinity in the renewal and sanctification of those who trust in Jesus. He comes to the heart in sanctifying power, excluding the evil and filling it with Divine love, when we believe the blood of Jesus cleanseth us from all sin, just as He comes in regenerating power when we believe for forgiveness, and are adopted into the family of God.

The first point to be recognized, as clearly set forth in

the Scriptures, is the fact that all Christians do possess the Holy Spirit. They have not only been brought under His influence, but they have received the Holy Spirit Himself. This is a truth which needs to be particularly emphasized. ' If any man have not the Spirit of Christ, he is none of His.' And the converse of this is necessarily true, that if any man belongs to Christ, he must have the Spirit of Christ. ' It is remarkable,' observes Professor Godet, ' that the Spirit of Christ is here used as an equivalent of the Holy Spirit in the preceding proposition.' Christ dwells in us by His representative the Holy Spirit, so that a Christ-possessed and a Spirit-possessed soul mean exactly the same thing.

When Ignatius was on his trial at Rome, he was asked by the Emperor, ' What is the meaning of your name, Theophorus?' (God-bearer). He promptly replied, ' He who has Christ in his breast '. And all Christians are God-bearers, whether they realize it or not. The unspeakably glorious mystery of an in-dwelling Holy Ghost is the possession of even the weakest and most failing child of God. The mistake has often been made of looking upon the incoming of the Holy Spirit as an experience subsequent to conversion, as an arbitrary bestowment rather than a necessary vitality. But the Scriptures plainly teach that the Holy Spirit is a universal gift to all believers, one without which they cannot be believers at all. At the same time, we must recognize the fact that to possess the Holy Spirit is one thing, but to be filled with the Spirit is quite another. Before Pentecost the Holy Ghost had been given to the disciples. Christ had breathed upon them and said, ' Receive ye the Holy Ghost '. But Pentecost made an unspeakable difference to them. The visible tongues of fire were only emblems of what had passed within. What new creatures they then became! How their gross conception of Christ's kingdom was purged away, and how they were raised from earthliness to spirituality! Their intellects were flooded with Divine light, their souls throbbed with Divine sympathies, and their tongues spoke so wonderfully of the things of God, that all who had known them previously were amazed, saying, ' What meaneth this? ' They were all raised to a new altitude; a new energy and force possessed them. Each one became strong as an iron pillar, ' the weakest as David, and the strong as the angel of the Lord '. They met together as the sincere but timid and partially enlightened followers of Christ, but they left the upper room full of light, and power, and love. They were now filled with the Holy Ghost as an all-illuminating, all-strengthening, all-sanctifying presence. The baptism of fire has consumed their inward depravity, subsidized all their faculties, and filled to the full each capacity with Divine energy and life.

' Baptized with ' and ' filled with the Holy Ghost ' are often convertible terms in the Acts of the Apostles, but it is instructive to note that they are not always so. The apostles received but one baptism, but they were ' filled ' with the Spirit over and over again. The baptism of the Holy Ghost was, and still is, a sort of initiatory rite to the life of Pentecostal service, and fullness and victory. Christian life begins at Calvary, but effective service begins at Pentecost. Before Pentecost there was not much service rendered by the apostles that was worth the name. But with the Spirit's baptism they entered upon a new phase of life and service. The analogy of the sacrament of baptism connects the baptism of the Spirit with a new era in Christian life. Pentecost, and the visit to Cornelius, when the baptism of the Spirit is spoken of, were not only historical events, but great representative occasions, which may be held to typify and signify the beginning of the Spirit-filled life.

Almost all prominent Christian workers, whose labours have been pre-eminently owned of God, bear witness to the reception of a distinct definite blessing which they received subsequent to conversion, and which inaugurated a new era in their spiritual life. If questioned, they would give different accounts, probably, of how they received this experience, and describe it differently, but they suddenly became bold, mighty, aggressive, and conquering. They had received their Pentecost, and the Holy Spirit was in them the fire of love, the light of assurance, and the unction of power.

As far as God is concerned, there is no reason why weary wastes of disappointing years should stretch between Bethel and Peniel, between the Cross and Pentecost. It is not the will of God that forty years of wilderness wandering should lie between Egypt and the promised land. In apostolic days there was generally a brief interval between conversion and the baptism of the Spirit, but new converts were introduced at once to this fullness of blessing, and taught to expect it as a positive, conscious, and present experience. Under the preaching of Philip in Samaria, many were converted, and ' when they believed they were baptized, both men and women '. The successive steps through which they passed are mentioned; attention to the word, faith, great joy, and baptism with water. But before they should be disheartened by difficulties and demoralized by defeat, Peter and John were sent unto them from Jerusalem for the special purpose of leading these newly-saved ones into the fullness of blessing. They prayed for them that they might receive the Holy Ghost, and they laid their hands upon them, and they received the Holy Ghost.

St. Paul's first question to ' certain disciples ', which he found at Ephesus, was, ' Have ye received the Holy Ghost since ye believed ? ' ' Jesus hath sent me,' said Ananias to the newly-converted Saul of Tarsus, ' that thou mayest be filled with the Holy Ghost.' How many backslidings would be prevented if we returned to primitive methods, and urged our converts to seek this experience at the beginning of their Christian life ! None can deny that the ordinary Christian in our Churches, weakened as he is by doubt and palsied by fear, with his worldliness and backslidings, far more resembles the condition of the disciples before Pentecost than after it. Who can read the Acts of the Apostles without coming to the conclusion that the Apos-

tolic Church enjoyed a much larger measure of the Spirit's
fullness than is generally experienced by Christians to-day.
We claim to be sharers in pentecostal privileges, and yet
how few enjoy the fullness of blessing which Christ is
exalted to bestow! If we are not filled with the Spirit, at
whose door does the blame lie? The question is not, ' Has
God given?' but, ' Have we received?' The might of God
was not exhausted in the day of Pentecost. That baptism
was simply a pledge and earnest of what God intends to
do for His people. We are still in the dispensation of the
Spirit, and the promise still stands, ' The promise is unto
you and to your children, and to all that are afar off,
even to as many as the Lord our God shall call ' (Acts ii.
39). The promise is as far-reaching and extensive as the
need, and means that by virtue of our new birth it is our
individual privilege or birthright to be filled with the Holy
Ghost. Each believer has the right to aspire to this, the
right to pray for it, and the right to expect it to-day.

It is interesting to note the graduation in the teaching of
St. John's Gospel. In chapter iii. we have the ' life ' in its
beginning—the new birth (John iii. 7). In chapter iv. we
have ' life abundantly '—' a well of water springing up '.
We fill our cup and drink, and keep on drinking from this
inexhaustible supply. Those who have learned to do this
shall never thirst. The well is for the supply of personal
need. But Christianity extends beyond the individual;
provision is made for the needs of those about us. Hence
we are taught in the seventh chapter that rivers of blessing
shall ' flow out ' from all believers who are filled with the
Spirit. ' He that believeth on Me, as the Scriptures hath
said, out of his belly shall flow rivers of living water.'
Blessing is promised here on a magnificent scale. Notice
its hugeness, its Godlike vastness! ' Rivers,' not a babbling
brook, or a streamlet; not even a river, but ' rivers '. What
Divine prodigality! In this experience, ' *Grace, not in
rills, but in cataracts rolls* '. If it means anything, it means
that there is no limit to the blessing God can send, through
the feeblest of His servants, if they are prepared to receive

what He is ready to bestow. There shall not only be fullness, but overflow. Spirit-filled believers carry life, and satisfaction, and gladness wherever they go. Their presence is life-giving, fructifying, refreshing, even as a river which blesses as it flows. ' Everything shall live whithersoever the river cometh.' The weakest, feeblest member of the body of Christ may be so instinct with the most vigorous life that there shall come forth from him a holy river-like abundance to the blessing of the souls of others.

Let us not confuse this fullness of the Spirit with any particular modes of blessing. Sometimes His coming distils as the dew, or it may be like the gentle summer shower, or as the mighty rushing wind. Some have an overwhelming sense of His presence; to others He comes, as it were, without observation, in a quiet gladness and confidence. Souls are brought into His blessing with as much diversity as sinners are brought into pardon and peace. He who blesses knows best what we need, and will adapt His gifts to us with infinite wisdom. But though His modes of coming vary, when He does come in fullness to the soul, all its chambers are filled with light, and not a taint of impurity remains.

We often speak and act as if it were the most difficult thing in the world to obtain the fullness of the Spirit, and yet it is certain that there is no blessing which the Father is so ready to bestow upon those who ask Him as this very gift. More willing is He to give the Holy Spirit to each believer than a mother to give the healing medicine to her dying child, or a father to give food and raiment to his soldier son who has just returned from the war. ' If ye, then, being evil, know how to give good gifts unto your children, how much more shall your Heavenly Father give the Holy Spirit to them that ask Him?'

CHAPTER XII

A LIVING SACRIFICE

THERE were two kinds of sacrifice in the Levitical economy
—of atonement and of acknowledgement. The former
found their fulfilment and their end in the Lamb of
Calvary, and are to be offered no more; but the sacrifice
of acknowledgement is perpetual in the Church.

Having clearly demonstrated, in the Epistle to the
Romans, that justification could not come by the law, the
apostle shows that the Gospel absorbs into itself the
sacrificial ideas of the law, spiritualizes them, and in their
most perfect form re-issues them as the rule for the Church
in succeeding ages. ' Present,' he says, ' your bodies,' not
your oxen, and sheep, and goats—the one great sacrifice
on Calvary hath swept these away for ever. The sacrifice
required now is not blood, but service, not death, but
noblest life. ' A living sacrifice' refers to the contrast
between the death of the victim under the law and the
life which is now to be presented to God; and to be consumed not by fire, but in doing God's will, and in the
service of humanity. Just as the Jew brought the body of
the dead sheep and laid it on the altar to be consumed, ' a
whole burnt offering ', so we are invited to bring our living
bodies, and present them to God to be consumed in a life
of perfect deeds and continual self-denial and devotion.

The term ' body ' is employed in this connection not
because it is the whole of man, or the chief part, but
bcause it is that alone which we can visibly offer to God;
and hence it embraces the whole man in the meaning of
the apostle. It expresses the same idea as the significant
ceremony which took place in connection with the consecration of Aaron and his sons to the priest's office. The
blood of the ram of consecration was placed first upon
the tip of the right ear, then upon the thumb of the right
hand, then upon the great toe of the right foot. ' The
boundaries of the man ', as Matthew Henry phrases it,

were thus claimed for God. The ear was marked first as
if to show that before using the hand or the foot we must
listen for the Divine Voice and only use them as God
commands, being deaf to all other voices that would call
us in other directions. It is indeed a solemn day in our
history when we recognize to the full the claims of God,
and bring not only our souls to Him for salvation, but
our bodies for sanctification and service.

We offer our bodies to God a ' living sacrifice ', when
in all the common actions of life we act with supreme
regard for, and distinct reference to, God and His will
concerning us; when, with all the sacredness with which
a Jew regarded the animals laid on the brazen altar, we
regard ourselves as belonging to God. Henceforth we exist
to work out God's purposes. ' Sacred to Jesus ' is inscribed
upon all that we possess, and all is kept sacredly for the
Master's use. We then practically recognize, in everyday
life, God's absolute proprietorship of body, soul and spirit,
and whether we eat or drink or whatever we do, we do
all to the glory of God. We resolve that Christ shall lead
us, plan for us, and have His way with us in everything,
in a word, that Christ shall possess our whole being and
reign supreme. The idea is that our whole life is to be
sacred—there is to be nothing secular in it. What cannot
be done for the glory of God is not to be done at all; and
what is done in every matter, from the least to the greatest,
we are to do ' unto Him '. The bells that jingle on the
horses of the wagoner's team are to bear the same inscrip-
tion as is blazoned on the High Priest's mitre, ' Holiness
unto the Lord ' ; and the shop-girl behind the counter may
offer as acceptable an offering to God as the priest by the
altar. That is the true sacrifice when we think as in His
sight, and will, and love, and act always in obedience
to Him.

Some say, ' Give us the morality of the New Testament,
never mind about the theology '. But the apostle devotes
the first eight chapters of his Epistle to building up the
doctrinal structure of the Christian faith tier after tier,

before he attempts any exhortation to Christian duty. He would teach us by this that all the practical is to be built upon the doctrinal; that, as Dr. Maclaren says, ' You cannot get morality without theology, unless you would like to have rootless flowers and lamps without oil '. Practical holiness is not something that begins by *doing,* but by *being.* It is not something to be manufactured, nor is it a mere question of imitation. A flower may be imitated, but we can always tell an artificial flower. Drummond compares a Christian and a mortalist to a living organism and a crystal. The crystal does not grow, it increases by accretions from without. The living organism grows vitally from within. The Christian works from the centre to the circumference, the moralist from the circumference to the centre. Holiness works from the heart to the surface. It is the outcome of Christ's own indwelling. When the apostle said, ' Christ liveth in me ', he meant more than the mere fact of Christ's presence— he meant that his life and service were the direct outcome of the unhindered working of Christ's indwelling. As the very life of the vine itself is in the branch, so Christ would live in us and manifest Himself in our mortal bodies to those around us.

Some writer has said, ' If the graces of the Spirit are within us, they will sometimes look out of the windows ', and if Christ really dwells in our hearts, it will not be long before He will be seen and felt in our thoughts, words and actions. As He lived we will live, as He ministered to others we will minister, as He was patient, thoughtful, unselfish, and kind, so will we be. We are to manifest in our daily walk that the very life of the Lord Jesus, which was poured out for us, has been communicated to us. ' Always bearing about in the body the dying of the Lord Jesus, that the life also of Jesus might be made manifest in our body.' Our life, measured by every standard of human measurement, may be very poor, weak and insufficient, but if Christ's life flows into us and through us, we shall not fail to make some contribution towards the accomplishment of His blessed purposes of love and mercy

to a fallen world. With our feet we shall then run errands
of mercy, with our lips we shall tell of His love and faithfulness, with our hands we shall do deeds of kindness and
tenderness; our whole being shall be employed in scattering
blessings of helpfulness and gladness all about us.

To increase by scattering and grow poor by withholding,
to save by losing and lose by saving, is the climax of
absurdity to a carnal heart, but it is a first and fundamental
principle of Christ's teaching. The taunt, ' He saved
others, Himself He cannot save ', was truth unconsciously
told. Jesus Himself could not become fruitful until, like
the corn of wheat, He had fallen into the ground to die.
His friends said He wasted His life. But was that life
wasted when Jesus was crucified? Who knows the blessed
gain of Christ's life through His sacrifice and death? Was
Mary's ointment wasted when she broke the vase and
poured it upon her Lord? What remembrance would it
have had if she had not poured it out, lost it, sacrificed it?
Nor can our lives ever become of much blessing to the
world until the law of self-sacrifice has become the pre-
dominating principle. As Dr. Miller says, ' The altar
stands in the foreground of every life, and can be passed
by only at the cost of all that is noblest and best. There
is more grandeur in five minutes of self-renunciation than
in a whole lifetime of self-interest and self-seeking '.

The Master's teaching is that we have to die to live.
Death is the gate of life. If we would save others, we
must sacrifice ourselves. Poussa, the potter, after many
efforts to make a set of porcelain worthy of the emperor's
table, despaired at last of making anything worthy of the
royal acceptance, so he flung himself into the furnace where
he was glazing his wares. The Chinese sages say that such
heavenly beauty never gilded porcelain before as made it
shine. They were writing more wisely than they knew.
' Except a corn of wheat fall into the ground and die, it
abideth alone; but if it die in bringing forth much fruit.'
The teaching is that that which cost nothing accomplishes
nothing. Service without sacrifice secures no results, no

achievement, no victory that is worth the name. If we would keep our life we shall lose it, but if we empty it out in loving service we shall make it a lasting blessing to the world. No high thing can be done easily or without cost. To be consumed in God's work as 'a living sacrifice' means burning up and burning out; the candle will grow shorter and the battery weaker. That is a true symbol of the consecrated life, which is inscribed on the tomb of Dr. Adam Clarke—a burning candle, with the superscription, 'I give light by being myself consumed'. We give light by giving up our lives to Him who loved us; we are consumed by the zeal of His house while we carry light and salvation to those from whom He died.

In the Gallery of Arts in Paris stands a beautiful statue, which has a strange and touching history. The sculptor was an unknown man, who lived in a garret and was very poor. He spent some of the best years of his life on this work, and after many disappointments and failures it was finished to his satisfaction. He cemented the parts together, and lay down to rest. But in the middle of the night he awoke with a start. A terrible frost had come over the city, and he was afraid lest his life's work should be marred, so he got up and wrapped what scanty bedclothing he had around his work to preserve it. He then lay down again and slept, but he never awoke. The next day he was not moving about as usual, so the neighbours burst open the door, and they wept when they saw how he had sacrificed himself for his work. They buried him, but his work still lives and will live, the wonder and admiration of all who behold it. Much like this will it be with those who have renounced themselves in order to glorify God and do good to men. When they are dead and gone their work will live, and some day rich and glorious reward will be given. Their work at present may be unrecognized and unnoticed. It may be like the dew which falls at night unobserved. Who takes any notice of it? But in the morning the beautiful result is seen on every blade of grass and the spray of every tree, and by-and-by the morning will dawn, the shadows

will flee away, and one of the sweet surprises of heaven to
those who have sacrificed themselves for their work will be
how much has come out of their poor efforts.

It is mercy that calls for duty and melts us into com-
pliance. After setting forth Divine mercy as never in the
world before—in its sovereign freeness, unfathomable
depths and glorious issues, the apostle says : ' By all that
through the inspiring Spirit I have shewed you, I beseech
you " Present your bodies a living sacrifice . . . unto God ".'
Such an appeal should be irresistible. It is as though
Christ Himself said, ' By the blood I have shed, by the
pangs I have suffered, by the life that I have lived, and
by the death that I have died, I beseech you present yourselves to Me '. How sweetly cogent : who can refuse ?

> Love so amazing, so Divine,
> Demands my soul, my life, my all.

CHAPTER XIII

WALKING WITH GOD

HOLINESS is not only a state but a way, and not only a way, but a highway, wherein the redeemed are to walk; and walking along that highway we shall always have Christ at our side.

We get into the highway of holiness by a definite act of consecration and faith, and walk upon the highway by continuous surrender and trust. Christ is the door, and He is the way. Walking with Him, we shall grow more and more unworldly and heavenly-minded, more transformed, more like Christ, until our very faces shall be radiant with Divine glory. As with Moses, who ' wist not that the skin of his face shone ' with the reflected radiance which it had received when he was in the presence of Jehovah, so from those who walk with God there emanates an unconscious influence which makes the ungodly tremble before them as Satan in *Paradise Lost,* when he saw the sinless pair in Eden, ' trembled to behold how awful goodness is '.

When the old Hebrews wanted to describe a man who reached their ideal in religious life, they used the simple but comprehensive phrase, ' he walked with God '. To them there was nothing higher than unbroken and unclouded communion with their Maker. That was, in their view, the secret of all holiness, and the New Testament has nothing higher than that to reveal. ' We all with unveiled face beholding, as in a mirror, the glory of the Lord, are transformed into the same image.' When we sit before the camera, and have our portraits taken, our picture is printed on the prepared film; but when we behold and continue to behold the image of Christ we become the camera, and His image is printed on our souls. The teaching is, that we become like those with whom we keep company.

' We say we exchange words when we meet,' says Professor Drummond, ' what we exchange is souls. And when our intercourse is close, and very frequent, so complete is this exchange that recognizable bits of the one soul begin to show in the other's nature, and the second is conscious of a similar and growing debt to the first. This mysterious approximating of two souls, who has not witnessed? Who has not watched some old couple come down life's pilgrimage hand in hand with such gentle trust and joy in one another that their very faces wore the self-same look? These were not two souls, it was a composite soul. Half a century's companionship had told upon them, they were changed into the same image.' What glorious possibilities are here suggested to those whom God hides in the secret of His presence? Who can think mean thoughts, or speak ungenerous words, in the presence of Christ? His mere presence must suggest immediately the right thing in the controlling passion, the subduing of pride, and the overcoming of selfishness. In His company, who could help but always be at his best, and if this influence is perpetuated, what could not life become? Walking with God implies at least three things :—

I. Companionship

We could hardly be said to walk with a person without a distinct sense of that person's presence. Was not this our Lord's promise to His disciples (John xiv. 21-24), and which Jude did not understand when he said, ' Lord, how is it Thou wilt manifest Thyself to us and not unto the world? ' It was altogether incomprehensible to them at the time, but afterwards they knew by blessed experience that He meant a real personal revelation of Himself, such as fills up the measure of the soul's need—a manifestation such as only the divinely illuminated soul can understand. Not a manifestation to our bodily senses; that would be impossible. God is a Spirit. Nor is it an intellectual revelation to perceptive reason. It is a manifestation to the inner consciousness of the believing heart, so that the Divine presence is as real as the sense of the presence of any human being. Christ becomes more really present than if we

could touch Him, or hear His loving human voice; forming
a companionship more intimate, sweet, and enduring, than
that of any earthly relationship, sweeter than that of a
friend with friend, of father and son, of mother and child.
Such communion is independent of matter or space or
time, it is a fellowship of spirit; as is all true friendship,
all love, human or divine.

Mr. Spurgeon once said that he never passed a single
quarter of an hour in his waking moments without a
distinct consciousness of the presence of the Lord.   How
much better this spiritual presence than a bodily presence
could be? A body is subject to locality, space, and time,
but now we can all have Him.   He is able to be with all
men always, everywhere, at the same time, even unto the
end of the world.   A late writer represents Christ as saying,
as He stood by the inconsolate sisters of Bethany, 'If I
had been away from the body, I should have been present
when Lazarus died'.   It was expedient that the bodily
presence should be withdrawn, that everywhere He could
come and go like the noiseless, invisible wind blowing the
wide world over wheresoever He listeth. A present personal
Christ solves every difficulty, and meets every requirement
of Christian experience.   We are not surprised that this
'Companionship of the Presence' has been described as
'the secret of secrets of the Christian life'.   We were outer
court worshippers before, but this is entering into the *inner*
court.   In this experience we know Him

> More present to Faith's vision keen
> Than any earthly vision seen;
> More near, more intimately nigh
> Than any outward earthly tie.

II.   Fellowship

When we speak of having fellowship with Christians,
we mean that we have union of hearts.   As we speak
together, heart goes out to heart.   Close friendship and
familiarity are always engendered when kindred spirits
walk much together.   They become communicative.   One

tells his trouble, and the other tries to console him under it, and then imparts his own secrets in return. 'Our fellowship is with the Father, and with His Son Jesus Christ.' No human friendship can be half so close and intimate as that which the lowliest Christian can have with his Saviour. In the New Testament the Christian's relationship to Christ is represented as a personal, conscious acquaintance with Him, which ripens into a close and tender friendship. Such is the mutual confidence now blessedly established between God and redeemed man, that even here on earth it is true that the Lord talks with Abraham, and through him, with all the family of the faithful, 'face to face as a man talketh with his friend'.

It has been well said, 'If you walk with God, you must talk with God, or you will soon cease to walk with Him'. But the intercourse is not one-sided. We must listen as well as pray. 'He that hath an ear to hear, let him hear.' On the one side we overhear God saying to Himself, 'Shall I hide from Abraham the thing that I do?' And on the other we hear the child of God complaining with hurt surprise, 'The Lord hath hid it from me and not told me'. We talk to Him, unbosoming our secrets, opening our hearts as we cannot do to any earthly creature. He talks to us quite as freely, allowing us to look into His heart and work as He explains the purpose of His grace, opening up with a friend's generous confidence the bearing of the yoke, the cross, and the thorn, upon our future, with Him and for Him.

What blessed revelations about the Father, the covenant, and the kingdom come daily to those who have formed with Christ this close, intimate and indissoluble friendship! There is a story told of a merchant prince of Glasgow, who was walking with a friend through the crowded streets of the city, when suddenly the companion heard him say, 'Oh, man, go on a bit. The Lord Jesus is wanting a talk with me'. It was so. He heard the whisper of the Holy Spirit, he felt the trysting tap of his Saviour, and dropped behind to let his soul go out in holy converse with his Lord.

Need we wonder that the friend was awed as he beheld the heavenly light in the countenance of the praying one, and that he lifted his hat as he watched that soul have its vision of open heaven and a present Saviour? Men who walk with God understand in their own real experience what it is to hear the soft footfall of the Divine Master, and to hear His whisperings in their hearts.

Many Christians are in too great a hurry to know this life of intimate fellowship with Christ. The Master comes to abide with them, but the place is too confused, and He withdraws. ' As thy servant was busy here and there, He was gone.' We must make time for meditative habits and communion with God. The soul grows thin in its activities. Says Dean Vaughan, ' Many a Christian's incessant action is the grave of his spiritual life '.

III. Progress

God never goes back, and if we walk with Him, we never shall. Walking is a regular, uniform motion, step by step, each one in advance of the last. It is not a rush, a leap, a spurt, but a steady progress from one point to another. Those who walk with God are not always speaking of palmy days and bright hours of fellowship that are gone. It is better with them now than ever in the past. They do not now and then climb to ecstatic heights and then descend into the valley of lukewarmness. The Christian life with them means steady progress. They go from point to point, from strength to strength, enjoying more, loving more, understanding more, receiving more, and giving more—in all respects they go forward. Such Christians are never satisfied with present experience, ' the goal of yesterday is always the starting-point of to-day '. Napoleon believed that still further conquests were necessary to the existence of his empire, that only by pushing its bounds farther and farther could he retain the territory he had conquered. In the Christian life this is certainly true. Going forward is the only security against going back. It is much to be born of the Spirit, and still more to be filled with the Spirit, but these experiences do not exempt us from the necessity of daily progress in Divine things. By slow degrees the likeness of Christ is perfected, as day by day we sensibly dwell in the secret of His presence.

Walking with God means step by step in the will of God. A man who carries a lantern at night does not see the whole path home; the lantern lights only a single step in advance; but when that step is taken another is lighted, and so on until the end of the journey. In like manner God lights our way. He makes one step plain, and when we take that, another, and then another. We have nothing to do with life in the aggregate. Each moment brings its duties, responsibilities, burdens, and needs. Our business is to live a moment at a time, and that moment for God. Dr. Kitto's advice is, 'Think not on a holy life, but on a holy moment as it flies. The first overwhelms by its immensity, the other sweetens and refreshes by its lightness and present stimulus; and yet a succession of holy moments constitutes a holy life '.

The question of great or small has no place here. We cannot live a life greater or grander than to be led step by step in all life's details by the Spirit of God. Progress always lies along the path that God chooses. The great thing is never to lose the thread of the Lord's leading. Obedience secures uninterruptedly the Divine presence. It is only in that path that we can 'go forward'. Those who have learned thus to walk with God so live in 'the practice' of the Master's presence, that it becomes impossible to live without Him, and gradually, little by little, the transformation into His likeness proceeds, even as by the Spirit of the Lord, until in the beatific vision we see Him face to face, and the likeness is complete.

CHAPTER XIV

BEULAH LAND

THOSE who have read Bunyan's immortal allegory will remember how he brings his pilgrims, before they crossed the river of death, into the land of Beulah. In that region they were ' clear out of sight of Doubting Castle '; the gates of the Celestial City were full in view, the sun shone by night as well as by day. They heard continually the singing of birds, and in their walks they encountered several groups of the shining ones. As they walked to and fro in this goodly land they found it to be ' a most pleasant, mountainous country, beautiful with woods, vineyards, fruits of all sorts, flowers also, with springs and fountains, very delectable to behold.' It may seem at first sadly at variance with facts to describe Christian experience on earth in such glowing colours, but there is a high and serene inheritance ' common to and for all pilgrims,' a promised land, towards which we are beckoned, where, as Dean Alford would say, ' Materially we are yet in the body, but in the spirit we are already in heaven—only waiting for the redemption of the body to be entirely and literally there.'

This experience so closely resembles heaven, that St. Paul took the term heaven and transformed it into an adjective-noun—' the heavenlies '—and used that term five times in the Epistle to the Ephesians to describe the region called by Bunyan the Land of Beulah. ' Blessed be the God and Father of our Lord Jesus Christ, who hath blessed us with all spiritual blessings in *heavenly places* in Christ.' See also Ephesians i. 20, ii. 6, iii. 10, vi. 12. When he uses the phrase ' heavenly places,' the apostle cannot be referring to heaven itself, because in chapter vi. 12 he speaks of our wrestling with ' principalities and powers ' and ' wicked spirits ' in the heavenly places, which must mean that it is an earthly experience, because there are no wicked spirits in heaven. There can be no doubt but that St. Paul had in view a sublime altitude of Christian experience in which the heavenly state is in us and we in it, so that literally in this present life we may live in a world of the unseen.

There is a story told by naturalists of a little insect that lives beneath the slimy pools, and makes for itself a house in the dark waters. In the centre of a bubble of air, which it inflates above the water and then takes down with it and moors to a little plant at the bottom of the pool, it lives. There, in its little world of light and air, it breathes, and builds its nest, and rears its young; dwelling below, and yet living above, and breathing the air of the upper world, while all around it are dark waters and slimy depths, and the creatures that come and go around its floating house of air. This illustrates in some measure what we mean by living in the ' heavenly places ' in Christ Jesus. As we walk through this dark world of sin and sorrow we have another world about us—a higher, sweeter, purer world; and while our feet tread the earth below, our hearts and heads are in the heavens, shut in with Christ. We are encompassed with a little world of light and glory which has descended from the skies—a kind of heavenly cloud in which we live and work like the little insect in its ethereal sphere. Was this not what the apostle meant when he wrote, ' Our conversation is in heaven '? Christians need not die to know what heaven is—

> The men of grace have found
> Glory begun below.

We need not anxiously inquire where the ' heavenly places ' are. It is enough to know they are where Jesus is. The expression refers more to the spiritual atmosphere than to locality. Heaven is a state as well as a place; and just in proportion as we abide in Christ, and live in communion with Him, do we have the earnest and first-fruits of the heavenly glory. The more God enters into our life, the smaller, the less startling will be the change at death. ' Weep not for me,' said a dying saint to his friends who stood weeping round his bed; ' I go to change my place, but not my company. I have walked with God on earth, and He is calling me now to walk with Him in heaven.'

> Though heaven's above and earth's below,
> Yet are they but one state,
> And each the other with sweet skill
> Doth interpenetrate.—FABER.

Canaan was to the Jewish people what the 'heavenly places' are to us. The writer of the Epistle to the Hebrews warns the Jews, from the failure of their fathers, not to fail to enter the true rest which was typified by their fathers entering Canaan. Some assume that Canaan is always a type of heaven, and that the rest spoken of eleven times in the chapters of the Epistle to the Hebrews refers to the perfect rest of the heavenly world; but the writer of the Epistle speaks of it as a present state—'We which have believed do enter into rest'—from which it is obvious that some other rest than that of the perfect rest of heaven is referred to. The Jews had supposed that Canaan was the true rest, but the writer of the Epistle shows that there was a higher rest, of which the temporal rest of Canaan was only a type. 'If Joshua had given them rest, he would not have spoken of another day,' yet another day is spoken of. Eight hundred years after enjoying Canaan, David urged the people, 'To-day, if ye will hear His voice, harden not your hearts'; from which it is evident that entering Canaan did not exhaust the meaning of the words, 'They shall enter into My rest.' That land was a type, but only a type, of the rest which God has provided for His people. Joshua gave the physical, but he could not give the spiritual rest. Only in Jesus, the greater Joshua, can the true, real rest be found. It is only when He Himself, who is exulted into heaven, comes by His Spirit so fully to possess our hearts, as that He is in us, and we in Him, that we of a truth reach the Beulah Land—

> Where dwells the Lord, our Righteousness,
> And keeps His own in perfect peace
> And everlasting rest.

'The river of the water of life, clear as crystal, proceeding out of the throne of God and of the Lamb,' is only a poetical description of the indwelling Comforter whom the Lord Jesus promised to send to His disciples, and through whom the Son of God would manifest Himself unto them, and the Father and the Son make their permanent abode with them. The bliss of heaven is of the same kind as the joy of Divine love shed abroad in the believer's heart, only it is more abundant. The Holy Spirit brings the joy of heaven with Him, and thus the saints above and the saints below drink from the same stream.

Beulah Land is not heaven, but it has been well described as ' the suburbs of heaven '. Another writer speaks of it as ' a little heaven to go to heaven in '. Mr. Wesley says, ' When the Holy Spirit fills the heart of a believer, He feasts the soul with such peace and joy in God as to blot out the remembrance of everything that we called peace and joy before.' This may seem strong language, but those who have felt the throb of love and gladness which accompanies the abiding fullness of the Holy Ghost can testify to its correctness. Speaking of the time when she entered this goodly land, Miss Havergal says, ' My whole life was lifted into the sunshine, of which all I had previously experienced was but as pale and passing April gleams compared with the fullness of summer glory '—

> I've reached the land of corn and wine,
> And all its riches freely mine;
> Here shines undimmed our blissful day,
> For all my night has passed away.

How meagre words are to describe the glory of this inheritance. To dwell where the beloved of the Lord dwell in safety by Him; where the sun shineth night and day; where the atmosphere is too transparent for doubt to live; where duty is transformed into delight; where the mouth is filled with laughter and the tongue with praise; where the soul finds rest from unsatisfied cravings; where triumph over temptation is complete and habitual; where, with joy unspeakable, we see the face of God in open enraptured vision, and are made glad by the assurance, deeply buried in the soul, that we do the things that please Him. ' To portray the blessedness of those who have reached these "heavenly places" is like representing the rainbow by a charcoal sketch.'

Oh, the sweetness of this inward spiritual kingdom! Oh, the depths of solid peace, the untroubled repose in God! What liberty is there possessed! What high, sacred, and pure enjoyment reigns! What fragrant breezes from the heavenly climes fill the air! What glorious unveilings of God to the soul! 'The light of the moon has become as the light of the sun, and the light of the sun shall be seven-fold.' The intenSe sweetness, the superior excellence, and the Divine glory of the perfect love of Jesus can never be exaggerated, nor indeed this promised land testify that even the glowing descriptions of Charles Wesley fall infinitely short of the reality—

> Rivers of milk and honey rise,
> And all the fruits of Paradise
> In endless plenty grow.

Does the country we have been describing seem to any of our readers like some far-off 'Eldorado', instead of a country nigh at hand? There is no need to regard it as a far-off land. No greater mistake could be made than to locate it as lying on the verge of the river, never to be reached until the close of our earthly career. It is nigh unto us.

The unbelieving Israelites remained forty years in the wilderness, when they might have entered their long-promised Canaan in less than a month. After they left Horeb, on the shores of the Red Sea, they consumed only eleven days before the vine-clad hills of Canaan were in full view, but 'they could not enter in because of unbelief.' 'Let us also fear lest, a promise being left us of entering into His rest, any of you should seem to come short of it.' We should say to those who, in God's mercy, have been led through the wilderness, and who are now on the borderland of the Canaan of God's perfect love, so that only the Jordan rolls between, 'Let us go up at once and possess it'. If

faith is the condition, and the only condition, we may enter
Beulah Land to-day. Hence the exhortation, 'Let us
labour, therefore, to enter into that rest.' The original word
for 'labour' is not a word signifying long and wearying
toil; it is radically the same as that found in the Septuagint
version of Joshua iv. 10, 'and the people *hasted* and passed
over.' The same idea is expressed in the hymn—

> O that I might at once go up,
> No more on this side Jordan stop,
> But now the land possess.

CHAPTER XV

SOUL REST

WHEN all our powers are harmonized, each with each, and all with God, the soul enters upon a condition of undisturbed rest which is beyond the reach of doubt and fear. Among the many characteristics of the spirit-filled life there is none more marked than this feeling of rest which is developed in our personal consciousness. We sing of rest beyond the river, but we must not transport to the other shore the things which God hath prepared for those who love Him on this side of the river. ' Eye hath not seen nor ear heard, neither have entered into the heart of man the things which God hath prepared for them that love Him.' These words are often quoted as though they had reference to the heavenly world. ' But,' says the Apostle, ' God hath revealed them unto us by His Spirit,' indicating clearly that the believer's heaven on earth is meant, not some experience beyond the grave. ' We which have believed *do enter* into rest.' This rest is described in the Epistle to the Hebrews as ' God's rest ' (Heb. iii. 11), ' My rest ' (Heb. iv. 1), ' His rest,' ' Christ's rest ' (Heb. iv. 10), ' a Sabbath rest ' (Heb. iv. 4, 9). In the same Epistle we are taught that :

I. SOUL REST IMPLIES CESSATION FROM OUR OWN WORKS

' For he hath entered in his rest, he also hath ceased from his own works as God did from His ' (Heb. iv. 10). Cessation from our own works does not mean ceasing from all kinds of work, for that is not true of saints either on earth or in heaven. We have no reason to believe that any saint or angel, or even God Himself, is ever inactive. He who enjoys soul rest is brought so intimately into sympathy with the Saviour that he is all aflame with zeal, ever hastening with quickened footsteps towards sinners dying in their sins around him. It is as a widely-known preacher quaintly expressed it, ' I enjoy that rest of faith that keeps

88

me in perpetual motion.' We are to cease to perform works with any such design as that of thereby saving our souls. Just so long as that constitutes the supreme object of our works, we are doing 'our own works'. But when the question of our soul's salvation is thrown entirely on Christ, and our works are performed out of love to God, they are not our works, but Christ's works—the result of His working in us to will and to do of His good pleasure. In one sense they are our works, because they are done by our own voluntary agency, but Christ is the moving cause of all that we do. True faith works love, and love does all for Christ. Faith in the great Atonement is the only basis of acceptance with God, apart from anything we can do. Faith sees salvation secured in Christ and ceases from compensative works, which by many are vainly wrought as a sort of offset against Divine forgiveness. As God did not rest until He had finished His creative works, so the Christian cannot rest until he ceases altogether from his legal works, and casts himself entirely upon the Saviour for salvation. Says Dr. Finney, 'The truly believing soul rests from it own works. It sees salvation secured in Jesus Christ, and has no longer any motive for legal works. It works not from self nor for self; but its works are from Christ and for Christ.'

In like manner we cease from our own efforts to live the Christian life. Many Christians live a life of resolution, instead of a life of faith in the Son of God. Those who trust to their own strength of purpose always find failure the result. The Gospel scheme is not fixing our will like flint, resolved to conquer or die. It is to commit the keeping of the soul wholly to Christ, and to cease from our own efforts. When we understand that it is not self-control, but Christ-control, we learn the secret of victory. The attitude of the believing soul is that of Peter's when he first stepped from the ship upon the waters of the sea, 'Looking unto Jesus.' Philosophy says, 'Keep your eye upon your enemies'; but the Gospel says, 'Eye Jesus only.' Weakness results from a constant survey of the difficulties and temptations which beset us. Power comes when the eye turns towards the angel Jehovah. Christ is our ' I am ' for every ' I need ' of the soul. He is the storehouse, and, as need arises, we must go to Him. He supplies need as it comes, but not until it does come, and as we draw upon Him. ' Human nature wants more—wants to feel its wealth, to finger its coin; but is it not better to leave it in the bank, and go there for it as often, and in as large sums, as we like? ' Such is the life of faith—having all in Christ, and receiving all from Christ.

Self-endeavour is the great danger. This, rather than ambition, should be styled, ' the last infirmity of noble minds.' First the sinner goes about to establish his own righteousness, and even when that has proved to be a dead failure, he will be found striving to be his own sanctifier. Some write out their vows and put them into their Bible as reminders of their solemn engagements with God. Others decide that they will give more attention to closet prayer, attend all means of grace, visit the sick, and be more watchful against sin. Thus many sincere souls spend years in earnest struggling, substituting a renewed covenant, when failure disappoints them, for faith in the all-sufficient Saviour. Christ is offered to us in the Gospel as our Wisdom, Righteousness, Sanctification, and Redemption; and just so far as we make effort to dispense with Him in any of these particulars, we set aside the Gospel and seek salvation by the works of the law.

We have heard a lady tell how, when she was newly married, because she had not had much domestic experience, everything in the home seemed to go wrong. She did her best, but such difficulties arose that she was almost in a state of despair. One day she was so much discouraged that she sat down and wept. She was aroused by a knocking at the door, and found a telegraph boy with a telegram announcing that her mother was coming, and immediately her care was gone. ' When mother arrived,' she said, ' I had no more anxiety, what I could not do mother could, and when she was with me I rested.' What

that mother was to her daughter Christ wants to be to us.
If only we could learn to meet every call, difficulty,
temptation and trial, not saying, as many do, ' I shall never
be able to go through it ', but saying, ' I cannot, but Christ
can, and He is with me ', we should be able then to sing,
with ever-increasing depth of meaning,

> Jesus, I am resting, resting
> In the joy of what Thou art.

II. IT IS REST FROM WORRY AND FEAR OF FUTURE ILL

CARE is such a foe to happiness, that when it enters the
heart happiness departs. Next to sin, it is the greatest evil
that can come into a soul. It hinders prayers, prevents
usefulness and defeats itself. The more the bewildered
bird beats about the cage, the less chance it has of getting
away. Fear and faith cannot keep house together. But
a life free from care is not for that reason a careless life.
In a certain sense we must be careful. Be careful to maintain good works is an apostolic injunction. The hymn
contains the right sentiment, ' Careful, yet without care,
I am '. One cannot be too careful when the care is to be
right and to do right. But when the care is burdensome
and distressing, we must learn to cast it on the Lord. Fore-
thought is commanded, but foreboding is forbidden to those
who are Christians. Misgivings about the providence of
God lie at the root of all wearying worry. The secret
tranquillity is trust. ' He that believeth shall not make
haste.' Christ has the programme of our best possible
future in His hands. His will is the blending of infinite
love and wisdom. If He chooses for us there can be no
mistake. What the hidden plan of our future may be is
no concern of ours so long as it is the will of God.' It
is sure to be right. Our only concern moment by moment
should be, ' Am I in the will of God ? ' If I am, then all is
well. ' All things work together for good to them that love
God,' though we may not be able to understand it. With
this confidence we can sing with Faber—

> Ill that He blesses is my good.
>   And unblest good is ill;
> And that is right that seems most wrong,
>   If it be His sweet will.

God governed the world well before we came into it, and He will be at no loss so far as we are concerned. He has taken better care of our past, and secured better results for the present, than we have deserved; why should we be anxious for the future?

> How can I ever careful be,
>   While such a God is mine?
> He watches o'er me night and day,
>   And tells me, 'Mine is thine'.

The lilies of the field He cares for, and we are of more value than they; also the birds of the air, and we are better than they. The very hairs of our heads are all numbered; which means that in all our matters, even as insignificant as the loss of a hair, God is interested; and it is in such cease-less and perfect care—infinite, tender, loving, and reaching to every possible necessity—we are asked to trust. ' Casting all your care upon Him, for He careth for you.' Alford's comment on this passage is precious, because his critical scholarship brings out an idea not expressed in the English Version, ' Casting (once for all, by an act which includes the life) all your anxiety, the whole of it, not every anxiety as it arises, for none will arise if this transference has been effectually made.' The idea is that where there is perfect trust there is perfect contentment with our providential circumstances. We can then thank God even for disappointments, because we know they are for some wise purpose; and in this habit of reliance on God, not by spasms of faith, we find the true solvent for care. Those who have not entered into this rest not only bear the evils of to-day, but often import from the imaginary future all sorts of evils to increase their discomfort and distress. Can we not all say, as the aged Christian said to his family when they gathered round his deathbed, ' I have had many trials and difficulties during my life-time, but half of them never happened ' ? This custom of crossing mountains before we reach them is most detrimental to Christian life. ' Sufficient unto the day is the evil thereof.' Strength is never promised in advance, but given day by day as the day's needs require. We do well to follow Charles Kingsley's counsel, ' Do to-day's duty, fight to-day's temptation, and do not weaken and distract yourself by looking forward to things you cannot see, and could not understand if you saw them.' As grace is needed it will be given. ' My God shall supply all your need.' When we wonder if our need can be met, we act as absurdly as the little fish which Mr. Spurgeon imagined as swimming up the Thames, and wondering if there would be water enough for it. One day at a time, and one thing at a time, is one of the secrets of a life free from worry. If to-morrow brings some new duty, responsibility, struggle or trial, let it be sufficient that ' our God will be alive to-morrow.' Little faith will bring our souls to heaven, but great faith will bring heaven to our souls.

> Ye fearful saints, fresh courage take ;
> The clouds ye so much dread
> Are big with mercy, and shall break
> In blessings on your head.

III. Rest from internal conflict, or deliverance from indwelling sin

Rest is cessation from strife or war. The children of Israel rested when they were freed from their enemies. Those who enter the rest of faith cease from their struggle with the flesh, or inbred sin, or depravity, by whatever name it may be described. All antagonisms to God are expelled from the soul and Christ reigns without a rival. Christ and sin can never exist in a state of partnership or affiliation. There is no war more distressing than civil war, and when a confederacy against Christ rages in the believer's heart, there is no possibility of rest. The strong man may be bound, but not being cast out, he makes desperate efforts to burst his bonds and reassert his supremacy in the household. The ' infection of nature ' within responds favourably to the temptations of Satan without. When the believer would do good, evil is present with him. It is to be feared that the majority of Christians are living in the seventh chapter of Romans instead of the sixth and the eighth. The tendencies to evil are so strong within them, and the contest with the flesh so distressing as to extort the cry continually, ' O wretched man that I am! who shall deliver me from the body of this death?' But the seventh chapter of Romans was never designed to be a representation of the ideal Christian life; it is rather a portrayal of the struggles of a convicted sinner seeking justification by the deeds of the law. The ideal Christian life is described in the sixth chapter, ' Knowing this, that our old man is crucified with Him, that the body of sin might be destroyed, that henceforth we should not serve sin.' Here we are taught that the purpose of the crucifixion of the old man is that the body, 'in so far as it is a sin body' (Meyer), might be destroyed, 'annihilated' (Cremer), 'done away' (R.V.). 'But now, being made free from sin, and become servants to God, ye have your fruit unto holiness, and the end everlasting life.'

The commandment is, ' Crucify the flesh with its affections and lusts.' ' If ye do mortify the deeds of the body, ye shall live.' To crucify and to mortify mean to put to death. The old man is not to be merely held down, but to be crucified until he is quite dead. Repressive power is nowhere in the New Testament ascribed to the blood of Christ, but rather purifying efficacy. When St. Paul said that he kept his body under and brought it into subjection, he made no allusion to the flesh, the carnal mind, but to his innocent bodily appetites. God does not propose to destroy our natural appetites, propensities and affections, but to take the sin out of them that they may be exercised rightly and properly, and always for His glory.

When John Wesley asked the German, Arvid Gradin, for his definition of full salvation he replied as follows :—
' Repose in the blood of Christ, a firm confidence toward God and persuasion of His favour, the highest tranquillity,

serenity and peace of mind, with a deliverance from every
(inordinate) fleshly desire and a cessation of all even inward
sins.' To every word of this hundreds can subscribe. It
is not our mere theory, but our experience. While conscious
of many errors, ignorances, infirmities and defects which
every moment need the merit of Christ's death, we claim
by faith the rest from sin which the great poet of
Methodism thus beautifully describes : —

> All the struggle now is o'er,
>   And wars and fightings cease,
> Israel now need sin no more,
>   But dwell in perfect peace.
>
> All his enemies are gone,
>   Sin shall have in him no part,
> Israel now shall dwell alone,
>   With Jesus in his heart.

Astronomers tell us that there is a point between the
earth and the moon where the action of gravitation
changes, and if we could hurl a missile with sufficient force
that it would reach that point, instead of coming back to
earth, in the superior attraction of the moon, it would rush
on with increasing velocity to meet it. This illustrates
human experience when ' the law of the Spirit of life in
Christ Jesus hath made us free from the law of sin and
death.' The natural tendency in us towards sin (the law of
sin and death) is not only neutralized when Christ our *life*
is fully apprehended (the law of the spirit of life) but under
the more powerful operation of the latter law the soul now
gravitates upward, every aspiration is Godward, and His
service is a luxury and a delight.

CHAPTER XVI

CHRIST'S LEGACY TO THE CHURCH

MATTHEW HENRY says 'that when Christ died He left a will, in which He bequeathed His soul to His Father, his body to Joseph of Arimathea, His clothes fell to the soldiers, His mother He gave to John, but to His disciples, who had left all for Him, He left not silver and gold, but something that was infinitely better—His peace.' 'My peace I give unto you.' Elsewhere this peace is described as the peace of God, because He is its source and origin. It is the peace which Christ had with the Father from the beginning, the peace in the heart of the Eternal, the stillness of eternity entering the spirit, causing a waveless, breathless calm. It lies not in the emotions, nor in the absence of the emotions. It is a peace not springing up in the course of nature, but handed down from heaven, and implanted in the believing soul.

Nothing for a moment broke the serenity of Christ's life on earth. Tempest and tumult met Him everywhere, until outwardly His life was one of the most troubled that was ever lived. But the inner life was a sea of glass. The highest tranquillity, serenity, and peace of mind were always there. It was at the very time when the blood-hounds were dogging Him in the streets of Jerusalem, that He turned to His disciples and offered them, as a last legacy, 'My peace'. If the meagreness of human language fails to convey to a blind man the vastness of that ocean which lies in the hollow of the Creator's hand how much more is its poverty seen when it attempts to set forth, in an inexperienced soul, all that is meant by God's perfect peace.

All Christians have peace *with* God, but this peace *of* God transcends every mind, every attempt of the strongest intellect, to realize its qualities and to describe it. Like the love of Christ, it 'passeth knowledge', or, as the apostle says in writing to the Philippians, it 'exceeds all understanding'.

Drummond describes it as ' the perfect poise of the soul ;
the absolute adjustment of the inward man to the stress
of outward things ;   the preparedness against every
emergency ;   the external calm of an invulnerable faith ;
the repose of a heart set deep in God '.

It is the deep tranquillity of a soul resting wholly upon
God, in contrast with the unrest and anxiety engendered by
a self-centred and worldly spirit.   Jesus called it ' My
peace ', in contrast with the hollowness of what the world
calls peace.   The world's peace is determined by outward
things, and is as changeable as external conditions.   But the
peace of God changes not.   It is not fitful and transient,
but an abiding and ever-increasing reality.   Ecstatic joy
fluctuates like the waves of the sea, but peace flows on
without interruption, like a river ever flowing and full.

> Like a river glorious
>   Is God's perfect peace,
> Over all victorious,
>   In its bright increase ;
> Perfect—yet it floweth
>   Fuller every day ;
> Perfect—yet it groweth
>   Deeper all the way.

It is easy to be tranquil when circumstances are
favourable, and when we are high up above trouble, but
the test is when we are in the midst of the waters, and
when the waves thereof roar and are troubled.   The peace
which Christ promises never fails.   Neither things present
can disturb it, nor life nor death dispel it.   It is abiding,
and not intermittent ; an unruffled under-current beneath
the ground swell of the believer's griefs and sorrows ; a
peace which exists independently of circumstances secure
and certain, which ' the world can neither give nor
take away '.

Says John Fletcher : ' I thank God I am not afraid of any
evil tidings.   My heart stands calm, believing in the Lord,
and desiring Him to do with me whatsoever He
pleases. . . . Thank God, I enjoy uninterrupted peace in
the midst of my trials, which are sometimes not a

7

few.' Such undisturbed repose of the soul is the promised heritage of all God's people.

It was out of a deep experience of this very peace that Bunyan in his allegory tells us that the crowning gift of Emmanuel, when he was in possession of Mansoul, was ' to ordain a new officer in the town. A goodly person he was. His name was Mr. God's-peace. This man was set over all the notables of the city of Mansoul—my Lord Will-be-well, my Lord Mayor Understanding, Mr. Recorder Conscience, the subordinate preacher Mr. Mind, and all other natives of this great and famous city.' ' Mr. God's-peace himself,' writes Bunyan, ' was not a native of the city, but came with Prince Emmanuel : he was a great acquaintance of Captain Credence and Captain Goodhope; some say they were of kin, and I am of that opinion too. This man, Mr. God's-peace, as I have said, was made governor of the town in general, especially over the castle, and Captain Credence was to help him there. And I made great observation of it, that so long as all things went in Mansoul as this sweet-natured gentleman would, the town was in a most happy condition. Now were no jars, no chidings, no interposings, no unfaithful doings in all the town of Mansoul. Every man kept close to his own employment. The gentry, the officers, the soldiers, and all in the place, observed their order ; and as for the women and children of the town, they followed their business joyfully, they would work and sing from morning till night, so that quite through the town of Mansoul now nothing was to be found but harmony, happiness, joy, and health.'

Well has Bunyan pictured in these words the effect of that peace of God which ' garrisons the heart and mind through Christ Jesus '. God's-peace and Prince Emmanuel come and go together. When Emmanuel was grieved away from the city, Mr. God's-peace laid down his commission and departed too. This peace is only known when Jesus is in full possession of the soul. Christ brings His peace with Him. ' These things have I spoken unto you, that in Me ye might have peace.' In Me—not through Me, out of, or from Me, but in Me. He, Himself, is our peace. Seek not the gift, but the Giver. If you receive the Giver you will insure all His gifts. Perfect peace will inevitably follow when Christ is welcomed to reign over the soul.

There is no surer sign that the keys of all the chambers of the heart have not been given up to Him than inward unrest, to be tossed to and fro, driven upon the waves of inward turmoil and trouble. This explains why so many Christians do not continually realize the peace and blessedness of which occasionally they have glimpses and enjoyment. Only at times does some wandering note from this diviner music stray into their spirits. The experience comes at few and fitful moments. When it comes, often it is a surprise, and when it goes it leaves no explanation. They wish for it to return and to abide, and ask eagerly how they may secure it permanently. There is but one answer: Perfect peace can only endure so long as Jesus reigns. Where Christ is enthroned there is always peace.

It is only when we are prepared to let Him takes His rightful place as Master and Lord of our whole life, that we can realize the fulfilment of the prayer, ' Now the God of peace Himself give you peace always by all means '. At all times, everywhere, and under all circumstances, we shall be kept in perfect peace. We shall know then, by a blessed and abiding experience, what the peace of Jesus really is, and share with Him the peace which He shared with the Father from before the foundation of the world.

Christ's peace is thus a sort of instalment of ' heaven's perfect peace ' that awaits all the children of God. Never lessening or stationary, but ever deepening and widening, it flows on year by year, and day by day, until it reaches the full blessedness of the stormless ocean of eternity.

CHAPTER XVII

JOY IN THE HOLY GHOST

THE question is often asked, ' How are we to keep our converts from lusting for the flesh-pots of Egypt, the leeks, the onions, and garlic of their former life? ' There is but one answer, the joy they have in God must surpass all the pleasures of sense. We read in the old myth that the Sirens sang men to death, but died themselves if they failed. When the Argonauts passed by them, Jason ordered Orpheus to strike his lyre. The enchantment of his singing and music surpassed theirs, and the Argonauts sailed safely by; whereupon the Sirens cast themselves into the sea and became transformed into rocks. We cannot make the Sirens fail unless we carry a charm with us greater than theirs. Joy must conquer joy, and music must conquer music; the Christian must have a music in his own soul far sweeter than any Siren-song of this delusive world.

There is certainly a general promise to all believers: ' Ask, and ye shall receive, that your joy may be full.' ' These things have I spoken unto you, that My joy might remain in you, and that your joy might be full.' Twice St. John mentions that the purpose he had in writing his Epistle was ' that your joy might be full '. Paul goes a step farther, and insists that joy is a Christian duty. ' Rejoice in the Lord alway, and again I say, Rejoice.' Evidently God means His people to be enthusiastic, buoyant, glad. A joyless Christian is a stumbling-block to the world and an offence to his brethren and to God. One of the chief secrets of the success of the early Christians was that they were filled with a gladness which was all-satisfying. Men judge of Religion by those who are considered to possess it, and they will embrace or reject it according to the manner in which it is exhibited before them. They are attracted more by radiant faces and over-flowing hearts than by eloquence or argument or any other human power.

When we show them something better than they have and carry about the advertisement of a gladness which arises superior to all circumstances, we shall win men for Christ. The joy of the Lord is our strength. The average type of Christian life will have to be raised before there can be any great advance of the Kingdom of Christ. Many of God's people have just as much gloom and depression and as many cares and anxieties as the people of the world. ' How is it,' said a godly minister to the writer recently, ' that we so very seldom meet with a really joyful Christian ? ' It is certain we do not find in our Churches so much of the exultant, exuberant joy which our fathers had. The absence of the rapture and triumph expressed in Charles Wesley's hymns too plainly indicates an imperfect acquaintance with Christ's great salvation. The reason why Christians are not overflowing with joy is because they are not filled with the Holy Ghost. ' The Kingdom of God is righteousness, peace and joy in the Holy Ghost.' When the blessed Comforter fills the heart of a believer, he opens such a fountain of joy within him, so sweet, so full and so lasting as to utterly extinguish all desire for base delights. ' I am dwelling,' wrote the seraphic Payson in one of his letters, ' in the land of Beulah, the celestial city is in full view. I can hear its songs ; I am gazing at its sunshine ; I am breathing its sweet odours. Oh, that I had only known what I now know twenty-five years ago ! I might have walked all my days in the light of Heaven.' The Spirit-filled Christian has an artesian well of joy in his heart, a miraculous spring opened in his breast, which fills, floods and overwhelms his soul with joy unspeakable all the year round. Common surface wells are soon dry, but artesian wells, even in dry weather, have plenty of water. ' Be not drunk with wine,' wrote the Apostle, ' wherein is excess ; but be filled with the Spirit ; speaking one to another in psalms and hymns and spiritual songs ; singing and making melody in your heart to the Lord.' The fullness of the Spirit is God's provision for the universal longing of our fallen race for some external stimulant. It is surprising to some that the fullness of the Spirit is several times in the Scriptures contrasted with fullness of wine, but contrast always implies some points of likeness. In both experiences there is exhilaration and elevation of feeling produced by an agent from without the man, entering and exciting his sensibility. To those who find life monotonous, who crave for a stimulant which will bring relief, some excitement from

The trivial round, the common task,

which often makes life so drab and colourless, the Apostle offers, instead of strong drink, which ends in the scorpion's sting, the joys of the Holy Ghost. His presence in the hearts of the people will 'set the pulses dancing, and thrill the jaded frame, and lift the spirit above the task-work of life and the dreary and hard conditions which make up the daily lot of multitudes.' Hence it is when the Holy Spirit comes to abide with us we burst into spontaneous singing.

All other joys are superficial, evanescent, transient, but the joy of the Holy Ghost is the possession of the Holy Spirit Himself—the perennial fountain of all blessedness. Such joy is quite distinct from happiness, which depends, as the etymology of the word indicates, upon what happens—outward circumstances, such as health, prosperity, gladness, favourable position, the surrounding of friends, and comforts. Depending as it does upon external circumstances, happiness, like the tide, ebbs and flows. It is subject to constant variations, sometimes calm and subsiding, at other times blazing up, a tumultuous feeling, a quick emotion, a lively passion. Joy, on the contrary is an internal condition; it arises from our inner being, it flows from the soul, and being a self-dependent spring within the heart, it is permanent and abiding. Life's changes and reverses, what we call trouble, crosses and disappointments, which sweep over our life's surface, do not produce a ripple on the face of the waters of this deep well. 'Your joy no man taketh from you.'

This joy is not so much ceaseless rapture, but a settled

quiet of the heart, the tranquillity of a soul poised in harmony with the Divine will—it is having Christ's joy fulfilled in us. The joy of Christ when on earth is seldom spoken of, but His whole life of obedience was His joy. Spiritual rapture is not found by seeking it; we find it as Christ did in doing the Father's will. 'True, pure joy,' says Amiel, ' consists in the union of the individual will with the Divine will, and in the faith that this supreme will is directed by love.' Such joy we share with Christ when we are filled with the Holy Ghost.

> We need not go abroad for joy,
> Who have a feast at home ;
> Our sighs are turnèd into songs,
> The Comforter is come.

CHAPTER XVIII

POWER FOR SERVICE

WE do not disparage other kinds of power, but for spiritual work spiritual power is the first and indispensable qualification. Christianity invites and consecrates every gift of God, and every grace and art of which man is capable. Nowhere does human ability find such sublime inspiration and such lofty exercise as in the service of God. All natural gifts are good, when lost in the great purpose of the Gospel, but they are perilous if depended upon instead of the Holy Ghost. The more gifts the better, if all are subsidized and sanctified by the Spirit of God; but, apart from absolute reliance upon Him, gifts may become a peril and a snare. Said the late Mrs. Booth: 'The history of the Church proves that just in degree as she has come to have the human she has ceased to have faith in the supernatural.' Paul writes: 'Our Gospel came not unto you in word only, but also in power and in the Holy Ghost.' And again he says: 'My speech and my preaching was not with enticing words of man's wisdom, but in demonstration of the Spirit and in power.' If numbers and prestige decline, it is vain to resort to external aids and appliances. The work is spiritual, and only spiritual power can accomplish it.

Nobody ever was or ever will be converted merely by the preaching of the Gospel. It is the Gospel applied and enforced by the Holy Spirit that saves men. Like the Arctic sun, it is possible to give light without heat. Clear views of truth may be set forth, but without the Spirit's unction no convincing power will attend their enunciation. Sinners will not be converted, nor will believers be quickened and blessed.

It is lamentable to see how frequently Christian workers take that one and essential condition of success, the presence and power of the Holy Ghost, for granted, while they spare no pains to secure all other elements of necessary preparation. No worker can be inspired to the maximum of possible service without the fullness of the Holy Ghost. The weakest, with this anointing, is stronger than the strongest without it. Not that the same results will follow in the case of all believers who receive the fullness of the Spirit. The same spark would issue variously according to where it fell. If it fell upon tinder it would blaze, if upon marble it would go out, if upon wet wood it would leave a scar, if upon water it would raise a hiss, if upon powder it would explode. And the same Spirit produces different results according to the temperament, mental constitution and spiritual capacity of those upon whom He descends. Peter becomes *all* Peter in the bold prominence of his peculiar characteristics, but he is not duplicated in any other apostle. John is himself and so is Paul, and so shall all be who are filled with the Holy Ghost. It takes this baptism to bring out a man's individuality. The Church is too much like the ' Milky Way ' in the heavens. Astronomers tell us that it consists of a conglomeration of small stars so insignificant in size as to lose their individuality. The baptism of the Holy Ghost will make a bright and particular star of each person who receives it. Our work and mission will differ from that of others in its special features; but filled with the Spirit we shall each be prepared for our own life's work, whatever that work may be. No man can be all that he might be without this priceless gift.

It was this Pentecostal baptism that prepared apostles for their work. What else could have prepared instruments apparently so inadequate for their stupendous task? One more difficult was never undertaken by mortals. They are entrusted with a work which is to turn the world upside down. Is it conceivable that a few rude unlettered fishermen can overthrow all the great Religions of the world? Will the hatred and prejudice of the Jew, the supercilious contempt of the Roman and the pride and profligacy of the Greek give way at the bidding of peasants of Galilee?

Within one generation Paganism was shaken to the centre, and Christianity had spread throughout the known world. Had the Church continued to grow at the same rate at which it increased during the first century, in all probability three or four centuries would have completed the salvation of the world. To men filled with the Spirit difficulties melted into empty air. There was no limit to their hopes, because there was no limit to their power. 'The weakest became as David, and the strong as the Angel of the Lord.' Their strength was not 'as the strength of ten', but as the strength of the Almighty. Nothing could resist the wisdom and the Spirit by which they spoke. Multitudes were pricked to the heart, and cried, 'Men and brethren, what shall we do?'

The mighty victories of the early Church were won in the power of the Holy Ghost, and this, and this only, is the essential of Christianity as an all-conquering power in the world. Everything without this avails nothing, but with this our weakness is linked to Omnipotence, and all things are possible. We know of nothing else that is needed. Our machinery is well-nigh perfect. We have wealth, social status, educational advantages, printing-presses, Bible and Tract Societies, and Christian legislation on our side. The whole world is open to us. Nothing is wanted for the grand consummation of our work in the world but the baptism of fire. Pentecostal power will bring Pentecostal results.

Is there not an experience for us, similar in kind and degree to that experienced by the apostles? We say similar in kind, because the real secret of the mighty change in the character and conduct of the apostles was not in the power of speaking with tongues, nor in the power to work miracles, but in the possession of the Holy Spirit Himself. Power dwells in a person, and that person is God the Holy Ghost. He does not hire out His attributes, as some vainly imagine; He comes to our hearts Himself. To receive Him in His fullness is to receive power. His gifts vary with the ages, sometimes bestowed, and sometimes withheld. His administrations differ according to the needs

of the Church and the times, but He Himself remains the
same. ' I will pray the Father, and He shall give you
another Comforter, that He may abide with you for ever.'
The same power must, therefore, be possible to us which
was received by the apostles on and after the day of
Pentecost. We are still in the dispensation of the Spirit.
The might of God was not exhausted at Pentecost. That
was simply a specimen day; an earnest and pledge of a
still fuller manifestation of God to men. The promise still
stands, ' I will pour out My Spirit upon all flesh.'

Have we not all known men who possessed this
wonderful gift? They seemed to be able to look into the
very souls of their hearers, and to talk to them with an
almost Divine authority and instantaneous effect. Some of
them were not profound thinkers or powerful speakers, but
they were wholly devoted to God, and full of desire for the
salvation of souls. When they spoke they seemed
surcharged with an energy which could not be called their
own. They had something which touched their tongue,
and enabled them to declare with astonishing effectiveness
and attractiveness the message of grace. It was like the
holy oil poured on Aaron's head, and which, running down
to the skirts of his garments, communicated to the whole
man a grateful fragrance. We have felt at a loss to account
for their influence, and have been compelled to confess
that the power they possessed was not human but Divine.
They had received that Divine enduement which is called
unction, the crowning gift of the Holy Spirit for service.
It is neither pathos, nor eloquence, nor psychological power,
nor mental force, but a subtle, mysterious, unaccountable,
and almost irresistible influence which only God can give.
No words can describe the gift, but it may be known and
felt by all.

The experience of the late D. L. Moody, of America,
is very striking. We give it in his own words: ' When I
was preaching in Farwell Hall in Chicago, I never worked
harder to prepare my sermons than I did then. I preached
and preached; but it was beating against the air. A good

woman used to say : " Mr. Moody, you don't seem to have power in your preaching." Oh, my desire was that I might have a fresh anointing ! I requested this woman and a few others to come and pray with me every Friday at four o'clock. Oh, how piteously I prayed that God might fill the empty vessel ! After the fire in Chicago, I was in New York City, and going into the Bank in Wall Street, it seemed as if I felt a strange and mighty power coming over me. I went up to the hotel, and there in my room I wept before God, and cried, " Oh, my God, stay Thy hand ". He gave me such fullness that it seemed more than I could contain. May God forgive me if I should seem to speak in a boastful way; but I do not know that I have preached a sermon since but God has given me some soul. I would not be back where I was four years ago for all the wealth of the world. I seem a wonder to some of you; but I am a greater wonder to myself than to any one else. These are the very same sermons I preached at Chicago, word for word. They are not new sermons; but the power of God. It is not a new Gospel; but the old Gospel with the Holy Ghost of power.'

Such is Mr. Moody's account of the anointing which made him what he was. Nothing else can make a man so powerful and glorious in his life and history. The wonder is that any Christian worker can be content to work without it. Much better would it be for the world if the Church would cease making weak efforts for its salvation, and wait upon God, until it is endued with this power from on high. With it we shall accomplish more in one year than in a hundred years of working in our own strength. If we spent half as much time in positive prayer for this anointing as is spent in thinking about it, there would not be workers enough to help those who would be seeking their way to Jesus. Prayer and faith are the indispensable conditions. ' There in the heavens is the residue of the Spirit; prayer taps the reservoir, and the outlet widens as we pray.' The disciples continued with one accord in prayer and supplication. Socrates said that his work in Athens was to bring men ' from ignorance unconscious to ignorance conscious '. Our first need is the consciousness of need. When this is realized we shall put our desires into one heartfelt petition for the fullness of the Holy Ghost, and not cease to present it until we have prevailed. ' Tarry ye . . . until ye be endued with power from on high.'

CHAPTER XIX

VESSELS UNTO HONOUR

An ancient writer has wisely said, ' There have been from the beginning two orders of Christians. The majority of the one order live a harmless life, doing many good works, abstaining from gross evils, and attending the ordinances of God, but waging no downright earnest warfare against the world, nor making any strenuous efforts for the promotion of Christ's Kingdom. These aim at no special spiritual excellence, but are content with the average attainments of their neighbours. The other class of Christians not only abstain from every form of vice, but they are zealous of every kind of good works. They attend all the ordinances of God. They use all diligence to attain the whole mind that was in Christ, and to walk in the very footsteps of their beloved Master. They unhesitatingly trample on every pleasure which disqualifies for the highest usefulness. They deny themselves not only indulgences expressly forbidden, but also those which by experience they have found to diminish their enjoyment of God. They take up their cross daily. At the morning's dawn they pray, " Glorify Thyself in me this day, O blessed Jesus ". It is more than their meat and drink to do their Heavenly Father's will. They are not Quietists, ever lingering in secret places, delighting in the ecstasies of enraptured devotion ; they go forth from the closet, as Moses came down from the mount of God, with faces radiant with the Divine glory, and visiting the degraded and the outcasts they prove by their lives the divineness of the Gospel.'

Such Christians are vessels unto honour—they are the aristocracy of nobility in the Church of Christ. They are precious and used for high purposes, and in this their honour consists. It was the custom in olden times that the King's servants in England were made nobles by their service. To be used by the King is the greatest honour.

Reputation and reward and other consequences of service are desirable, but nothing is greater and grander and more blessed than the Master's service itself. Dishonoured vessels are those that are laid aside because not meet for the Master's use. Every man must settle for himself to which class he belongs.

That we may make no mistake in the matter, let us note some characteristics of those who are vessels unto honour.

In 2 Timothy ii. 20, 21, St. Paul mentions three. The ' vessel unto honour ' is ' sanctified ' ' meet for the Master's use,' ' prepared unto every good work.'

1. SANCTIFIED.—' The words of the New Testament,' says Archbishop Trench, ' are eminently the rudiments of Christian theology, and he who will not begin with a patient study of these shall never make any considerable advance.' Luther went so far as to say, ' Divinity is the grammar of the Holy Ghost '. The word ' sanctified ' is one of our commonest expressions, but have we taken the trouble to inquire into the special significance of the term as it is used in the New Testament? Sometimes the word is translated ' hallowed ' and sometimes ' holy ', but the fundamental ideas are exactly the same, separation and purity. In the Old Testament the term meant to be set apart for sacred purposes. It was used of the firstlings of the Hebrew flocks and herds, as being animals taken out from the rest set apart for God, to be laid upon His altar. It was used of Jerusalem the Holy City, and of its Temple, of the Temple furniture and of the priests who officiated there. They were set apart from common uses and devoted to high, sacred, and godly ones. But in the case of Aaron and his sons, who were set apart for the priest's office, more was required than that they should be separated and sacred persons. Before they entered upon their duties the ram of consecration was brought, its blood was applied to the extremities of their persons as signifying that the whole man needed to be purified. Then the anointing oil was put upon their bodies and garments, and for seven days these ceremonies were repeated. The plenteous ablutions, the

sprinkling of the blood, and the prepared white garments
were intended to symbolize the need there is of purity
before any can be ' meet for the Master's use '. The Apostle
had probably the services of the Temple in his mind when
he mentioned as the first qualification for ' a vessel unto
honour ' is that it be ' sanctified '.

The root thought of sanctification is separation. A man
sanctifies himself when he separates himself from all that
is evil and impure, and dedicates his whole heart and life
to the doing of the will of God. In this sense it is a
personal and definite act. He yields himself to God in a
spirit of entire submission. The surrender of ourselves to
God must be entire—including body, soul, life, talents,
reputation—everything. These are to be used when, where,
and as God demands, and only thus. It includes being,
doing, and suffering. The soul in this state of
abandonment cries :—

> Here I give my all to Thee,
>   Friends, and time, and earthly store ;
> Soul and body Thine to be,
>   Wholly Thine for evermore.

We are not entirely the Lord's unless we have settled
once for all that in will, in affection, in purpose, in honest
use of capacities and resources and all things, we will be
His for ever. Such a dedication is not sanctification, but
it is one element in it, the human element, and it prepares
the way for what remains. We have now come to the
Divine aspect of the work. In order that our sanctification
may be complete, God has to effect that cleansing, that
thorough renovation of our moral nature, which is promised
in the New Testament Covenant, and for which provision
has been made in Christ. Dedication is our duty, cleansing
is God's work, and He will accomplish His work directly
we perform our duty. It was for this St. Paul offered that
sublime prayer on behalf of the Thessalonians : ' But may
the God of Peace Himself sanctify you wholly ; and may
your spirit, soul and body, be preserved entire without
blame in the coming of the Lord Jesus.' (Ellicott.)

To be sanctified wholly is to be delivered from whatever is contrary to God in the soul, and to be hallowed in every faculty, propensity and power. Then the Apostle uses another peculiar term, which is found only once in the New Testament, in the Epistle by St. James i. 4, 'That ye may be perfect and entire, wanting nothing.' The word 'blameless' is the same exactly as that translated 'perfect and entire', and then immediately expounded 'wanting nothing'. The reference is again to the sacrifices under the old dispensation. A lamb to be perfect needed to have all its parts and members, and nothing else—no excrescence. It might be larger or smaller, younger or older, fatter or leaner than another lamb, but if it had all its members without any defect, and no excrescence, it was perfect according to the Law. And the Christian who possesses all the graces of the Spirit, none lacking, and without their opposites in any degree, may be preserved entire or complete, without blame, unto the coming of the Lord Jesus. The God of Peace 'Himself' will do it. The word 'Himself' is added to emphasize the fact that it is God's work to cleanse the soul from sin, and not ours. Eternal discouragement would overwhelm us if it depended on human effort. But all the difficulties vanish when God undertakes. It will help us amazingly to keep the truth before our minds that the God of Peace who has begun the work of grace in our hearts will Himself complete the cleansing. There need be no long interval between our surrender and this putting forth of the Divine power in the removal of our inward pollution. When our all is on the Altar, nothing else is required, but that we trust Him to do what He is able and willing to do. He will cleanse and keep clean those who trust Him fully. The phraseology of the Apostle's prayer implies that the work of cleansing is an instantaneous one. The verb 'sanctify' is in the aorist tense, which denotes a single momentary act. Sanctification is not intended to make us meet for the next world only, but to fit us for God's service in this present life, and to enable us to glorify Him to the fullest extent possible, according

8

to the opportunities and responsibilities of to-day. A little girl was reading the Beatitudes, when she was stopped and asked, 'If you could choose, which of these would you prefer to have?' 'I would rather be pure in heart,' she replied. On being asked the reason, she said, ' Because if I could obtain that I should possess all the rest.' The child was right. When we are sanctified, we are meet for the Master's use, and prepared unto every good work.

2. MEET FOR THE MASTER'S USE.—Meetness signifies fitness. To be 'meet' is to be just the thing—exactly adapted for the purpose. You want to convey a pure spring of water to your dwelling. You find upon your premises pipes which would serve as channels through which to conduct it, but you examine them and say, 'they are not fit for use, they are corroded with rust and covered with dirt '. Because they are not ' meet ' for use they are laid aside.

We are channels through which Divine grace is conveyed to men's souls. But if the channel is choked by pride, by low and sinister aims, by selfishness and earthliness, and by other hidden evils, how can we be used by the Master? When these are taken away, what a full tide of heavenly life might pour along and carry blessing to all around.

M'Cheyne wrote to a brother minister : ' How diligently the cavalry officer keeps his sabre clean and sharp. Every stain he rubs off with the greatest care. Remember, you are God's sword. A holy minister is an awful weapon in the hands of God. It is not so much great talents that God blesses, as likeness to Jesus.'

Does not all experience teach that holiness and usefulness are linked together. There may be exceptions, but this is the rule—whom God sanctifies for His work, He honours with success. It is not intellect, however brilliant; it is not genius, however wonderful; it is not eloquence, however captivating, that accomplishes the most good in the world. Simple goodness, holiness of life, and entire consecration, will furnish a power with which no human skill can compare. There may be showy public outward activity, without holiness, but there is little satisfactory result. We may work for God when God does not work with us. No man is fit for the Master's use, in the highest sense, except on condition that he is consecrated and pure. This explains why many professing Christians are not used in Christ's service, except on the poorest outward business, some kind of secular work tacked on to spiritual work. That is all they are fit for. As. Dr. Maclaren says, ' You cannot make men-of-war's masts out of crooked sticks '.

Personal holiness is the first tribute we owe to the Spirit for the Master's use; and we cannot offer him acceptable service until this is paid. A Roman historian tells of one who sent a present of a diadem to Caesar, while he was yet rebelling against him. Caesar returned it, with the admonitory reply, ' First yield obedience, and then make presents '. The spirit and truth of this message is addressed to every Christian. In vain we sing : —

> Bring forth the royal diadem,
> And crown Him Lord of all,

while we exempt anything, no matter how trifling, from the dominion of Christ. But when we are entirely set apart for God's service and will, and cleansed from the defilement of sin, we are always ready for use.

In our hospitals, the instruments used in operations are constantly kept in antiseptics, that they may not carry the slightest contagion to the open wound. We cannot touch the open and festering wounds which sin has caused, without injury to ourselves and others, unless we are, moment by moment, realizing that the blood of Jesus cleanses us from all sin.

While it is true that the efficiency of an instrument depends upon him who uses it, and that in Christian work ' the excellency of the power ' is of God, and not of us, it is also true that the adaptation of the instrument has something to do with the result. The clearness and elegance of writing depends in part upon the pen used. Even the touch of genius could not transform the marble into a thing

of beauty without proper tools.   There is a sense in which
the poet was right who said :—

> Not God Himself can do best work,
> Without best men to help Him.

This is neither irreverence nor heresy.   God works
through human instrumentalities, and if the instruments
are not ' meet ' or fit for His use, there will be a blank
or a blur where there ought to have been something
beautiful.   It is a wonderful thing that God should offer
man the glory and honour of sharing in His work, but that
He does so is beyond all doubt.

Christ is the True Vine, and we are the branches.   But
a vine does not bear fruit, except through the branches.
This is why He says, ' Every branch that beareth fruit, He
purgeth ', or cleanseth it, ' that it may bring forth more
fruit '.   To bear ' *much* fruit,' the branch of the vine must
be quite sound, and without rottenness, free from mildew
and blight, and fully cleansed from the parasites which
would destroy its beauty and verdure.

We do not wish to be understood as saying that
Christians cannot be useful in any degree unless they are
fully consecrated.   Every true Christian is of some service
to the Master, but for His highest purposes it is the cleansed
vessel that is used.   Here, for instance, is a machine, well
designed, and able to accomplish a given result.   But some
of its parts are out of place; some of the wheels are
clogged; and there is friction between the parts.   It is
doing *something,* but if it were in complete order, how
much more would it accomplish !   Here is a fruit tree, well
shaped and planted in a good soil.   It bears some fruit,
but it is untrimmed, and useless shoots are drawing away
its life.   Worms are at the root, or concealed in the bark.
Let the tree be put into good condition, and how its
branches bend under the burden of luscious fruit.   Not only
does it bear more fruit, but the quality is better.   So with
the Christian; he is useful with a little light, a little grace,
a little power, but we well know that if the grace were all

transforming and sanctifying, his usefulness would be vastly increased.

The Lord has need of us. There is no more spiritual and mysterious truth than that Christ our Head is actually and entirely dependent upon the members of His body for the accomplishment of His purposes of mercy towards a perishing world. Partnership in His saving work is the crown and highest glory to which any Christian can aspire. Would we be prepared for the maximum of possible service and blessing? Surely this is the ambition of every child of God. The answer is, ' If a man purge himself he shall be a vessel unto honour '. If we have failed in the past, it is not because of lack of talent or human ability. Is it not rather because our hearts have not been cleansed from sin?

3. PREPARED UNTO EVERY GOOD WORK.—This last characteristic means readiness for all sorts of service. The teaching is that holiness is the source of every kind of human excellence. It sets to work all our powers and in the best possible directions. It means the sanctification of hands, feet, brain, temper, pocket, the whole man inwardly and outwardly. The desire and aim then is to make a ' good work ' of whatever is given us to do, and to do it in the best and most perfect way, according to our light and knowledge; let it be the painting of a picture, the sweeping of a room, the managing of a business, or the preaching of a sermon. The meanest service is ennobled by its lofty motive when we work under the inspiration of the Cross. In estimating the value of Christian work we often think too much of our efforts and too little of our spirit and life, but character is really of more importance than our activities. ' Words have a weight,' says Thomas Carlyle, ' when there is a man behind them,' and when behind our efforts there is the fragrance of a holy and consistent life our labour cannot be in vain. ' Holy living is the rhetoric that tells best in this age of facts.' The measure of our holiness is the measure of our power. By this means and this only are we ' prepared unto every good work '.

Let us note the word ' every ' because we shall be many-sided when our hearts are cleansed from all sin. We are in danger of limiting our conceptions of duty to some particular sphere, repeating one note instead of a full chord; but the world is wide, and human need is great, and the best servants are the servants of all work. They are always on the alert for opportunities to do good, and ready, even if the call comes suddenly, as it often does. It is not with them as with many who are not living with their loins girt, and who often let their opportunity pass before they have pulled themselves together. It is a grand thing to be 'prepared unto every good work'—always ready. Chrysostom interprets the words to mean 'ready for every emergency which would add to the glory of God, ready even for death, if needs be, or any other painful witness'.

After the Seraphin had laid the live coal upon the lips of Isaiah, and had said, 'Lo! this hath touched thy lips, and thine iniquity is taken away, and thy sin purged', he heard the voice of the Lord saying, 'Whom shall I send and who will go for us?' Isaiah's glad and immediate response was, 'Here am I, send me'. In the same spirit we shall leap forward to fill positions of duty, honour, and danger, when our hearts are purified from self and sin.

CHAPTER XX

CONSECRATION

SOME writers of advanced Christian experience magnify the will and emphasize the importance of absolute submission, while others urge faith as the condition of blessing. Both are right. Perfect trust cannot exist without complete surrender. Nor can we surrender our will to One whom we cannot trust. Lady Maxwell could pray, ' Put a thorn in every enjoyment, a worm in every gourd, that would prevent, or in any measure retard my progress in Divine life '. And when we can say, from our inmost heart, ' I am willing to receive what Thou givest, and to want what Thou withholdest, and to relinquish what Thou takest, and to suffer what Thou inflictest, and to be what Thou requirest, and to do what Thou commandest. Have Thine own way with me and mine in all particulars,' we are not far from the Canaan of God's perfect love.

This full surrender is consecrated. It means an entire willingness on our part to be, to do, and to suffer, all that God wills. We use the word 'consecration' not because it is the best word, but because it is the word in most common use and the word most likely to be understood. What repentance is to justification, consecration is to entire sanctification. Just as repentance towards God must precede faith in the Lord Jesus Christ in the case of those who seek Divine forgiveness, so unconditional surrender is the indispensable condition of trusting Christ as a Saviour from indwelling sin. Some think they must struggle and make great effort, but faith does not come as the result of effort. It rises up spontaneously in the soul when the hindrances are removed. Unbelief has always a moral cause—unwillingness to do the will of God in some point. The difficulty is not with our faculties, nor with evidences, but with our moral state, our disposition to follow un-hesitatingly where the truth leads. Faith becomes as natural as breathing when we dethrone our idols. Nearly all the difficulty in reference to the faith which leads the Christian into full salvation is because of a reluctance to sell *all* to obtain this ' pearl of great price '.

Purity of heart can never be given or retained apart from a total, complete, and absolute abandonment of all sinful and doubtful practices and the acceptance and approval of the will of God. We must make ourselves over to God, and all that we have, to be used only for His glory, and in accordance with His will. As faithful stewards, we must be content to live only to carry out the wishes of Him to whom we belong. Under the old feudal system of personal homage, the vassal declared his submission and devotedness to his lord with uncovered head, ungirt belt, sword and spurs removed. Kneeling he placed his hand between those of his lord and promised to become his man henceforth, to serve him with life and limb and worldly honour, faithfully, loyally. He sealed it all with a kiss. Something of the solemnity, completeness and personal transfer of this old-time custom is an act of the soul's submission and transfer to Christ. It is a real inward and outward transfer of self to God. It implies a surrender of our will at every point—the unconditional acceptance of His will as the rule of our life for ever.

Not that our will is to become in any sense inoperative or dead : ' Union of the human will with the Divine is a very different thing from the extinction of the human will. A will, a proper and effective will, is essential to humanity. Man without a will ceases to be man. The perfection of man's nature does not consist in the extinction of his will, but in its union with God's will.' Such are the wise words of Professor Upham, to which we heartily subscribe. Some persons talk of their advanced experience by saying they have no will, but no degree of grace supersedes the use of our will faculty. God has made the will the hinge on which our destiny turns, and on its freedom rests our responsibility. The true doctrine is that our will must be subordinate to the will of God. Remaining in all its energy, our will must coincide and harmonize with the supreme will of God.

'Thy will be done in everything,' must be our attitude if we would enter into rest. Not that we are asked to disregard entirely our own welfare. Self-love is implanted in our nature, and, like the will, is essential to human individuality. If self-love were destroyed, there would be nothing to which God or man could appeal. Neither threatening nor promise would influence such a soul. Bishop Butler makes an important distinction between self-love and selfishness. Selfishness is self-love without regard for the will of God or the well-being of others. Self is exalted into the supreme law of action. It is this self that must be crucified before there can be a complete resurrection unto life. Christ, and not self, must occupy the centre of our being. St. Paul could never have said, 'I am crucified with Christ, it is no longer I that live, but Christ that liveth in me' (Ellicott), had self been still alive disputing with Christ the throne of the soul. Self had been nailed to the cross, and Christ had taken the supreme place in the soul. Octavius, who had been one of the three rulers of the Roman Empire, thought it best in the interests of peace that the world should have but one ruler, so, styling himself Augustus, he became that ruler by the defeat of Mark Antony. It was found that to have more than one ruler only provoked strife, and it is certainly for our soul's peace that there should henceforth be but one sovereign. We must choose between Jesus and the Barabbas of self. At the Keswick Convention, one who had been a Christian many years, described the nature of the blessing he had received in the following words:—'I had heard of Christ being King. Well, He had reigned in me, but it was only as a constitutional Sovereign. I was Prime Minister, and I did a good deal of the work myself. Then I found that He must be absolute Monarch. And so now He is.' Happy indeed are those who can shout over the accomplished fact in their experience,

None of self and all of Thee.

To those who enter upon the work of consecration in real earnest God will make demand after demand until the self-life is exhausted. Often there is some last rallying point where self is entrenched as in a stronghold, and when that point is surrendered the victory is complete. Abraham might have been willing to give up every other thing he possessed, but if he had not been willing to give up Isaac, all else would have been useless. ' It is our Isaac God wants. Many Christians have something they are holding on to which the Holy Spirit tells them they must let go. They have got their Isaac just as the young ruler had his possessions. God has made clear the subject of surrender, but they are unwilling to receive the light and to follow it. Some call the struggle which ensues spiritual conflict, but it is really spiritual rebellion. It may be a trifling thing that we exempt from the dominion of Christ, but it is not a small matter if we hold on to it in antagonism to God's will. It is the battle-ground between self and the Saviour and the test whether or not Christ shall reign. How we have heard persons argue, ' But this is such a trivial matter, God cannot require this', but all the time that was the point of controversy. It may be some adornment that has to be discarded, or some self-indulgent habit. Oftener it is some duty that has to be performed, some association to be broken from or some doubtful thing that has to be given up. ' Reign, Lord Jesus, over all but this,' is the real language of the unyielding heart, but before blessing comes there must be total, complete and unconditional surrender. Miss Havergal writes: ' It was on Advent Sunday, 1873, that I first saw the blessedness of true consecration. I saw it as a flash of electric light, and what you see you can never *un*see. There must be full surrender before there can be full blessedness. God admits you to the one by the other.' ' Keep this short and complete saying,' says Thomas à Kempis, ' Forsake all, and thou shalt find all,' which is in exact accord with the Master's teaching, ' He that saveth his life shall lose it, and he that loseth his life for My sake shall find it.'

When the will gladly makes this unconditional surrender it will not be long before the Christ-life will take the place of the old-self-life, and the believer will be able to reckon himself ' Dead indeed unto sin, but alive unto God through Christ Jesus our Lord '. An interval may elapse between full surrender and complete blessedness. The fullness as well as the intermediateness depends upon the faith of the soul in the Divine promise, but when the self-life dies the chief hindrance to faith is removed. Possibly the temptation will come that perhaps there is something not given up of which we are not conscious. You do not know all your heart, hence you cannot know that you have fully surrendered. But when the will is yielded, it includes all we know and all we do not know. If nothing less than living up to full life will suffice, nothing more is required. When we are not conscious of withholding anything from God, and are perfectly willing to receive the light and follow it, we may count the matter of consecration as settled.

A story is told of a Christian who once said, ' I often hear ministers say we must consecrate all to God unreservedly and unconditionally, if we would obtain the experience of full salvation. Now I confess I do not understand this. Did I not consecrate all to God when I first embraced religion? and that is all I can do.' 'Let us see,' replied the minister to whom he spoke, ' whether you have done all you can. Have you any pride?" ' Yes.' ' Has not that pride its object?' ' Certainly,' he said, after a short pause. ' Have you any selfishness?' ' Yes.' ' Has not that selfishness its object?' ' Well, I suppose so.' ' You know in what you desire to please self rather than God?' After a few moment's hesitation, he answered, ' I think I do.' ' Have you any undue love of the world?' ' I have.' ' Has it its object?' ' You need say no more. I see the point clearly. Pray for me '; and he went home to search his heart, and surrender in a consecration much more intelligent and discriminating than was possible when he first sought the Lord.

CHAPTER XXI

SANCTIFYING FAITH

THERE is this difference between consecration and entire sanctification—the one is what we do ourselves by Divine aid, the other is what God does in us. Consecration is our voluntary act in which we give our all to God, while entire sanctification is a work wrought in us by the Holy Ghost. There may be entire consecration without entire sanctification, but there cannot be the latter without the former. The act of consecration must be followed by definite prayer for a clean heart, and then the act of faith by which we receive what we ask for. In answer to our prayer and response to our faith God will put forth His power, and we shall be changed in a moment from indwelling sin to indwelling holiness. We are saved by grace. Just as over the blessing of justification, God has written over entire sanctification ' to him that worketh not.' Works have no more to do with the sanctifying of the soul than they have to do with the justifying of the soul. Faith is the condition in the one as well as in the other. There are many passages which expressly teach this. ' Purifying their hearts by faith.' ' An inheritance among them that are sanctified by faith that is in Me.' Many others might be quoted to the same effect. The real difficulty we find in presenting the salvation of God to the inquirer who is seeking forgiveness is this way of faith. We cannot make him see it is of faith and of faith only. Hence his groans, his tears, his weary efforts to mend his life, and in some measure to fit himself for God's acceptance. When at last the way of faith is revealed to him by the Holy Spirit he soon finds peace with God and the work is done.

Exactly so is it with sanctification. It is only when we cease from our own efforts and trust in Christ alone that blessing comes. The faith by which we are sanctified is the same exercise of the mind and heart as that which brings forgiveness, only having respect to different promises and other aspects of the redeeming work of the Lord Jesus. Works require time for their execution. Faith, on the contrary, is an act of the soul. In a moment the soul, by the exercise of faith, can ' wash and be clean '. Writing to his brother Charles, in the year 1766, John Wesley said, ' Insist everywhere on full redemption received now by faith alone. Press the instantaneous blessing.' On another occasion he wrote, ' To talk of this work as being gradual would be nonsense, as much as if we talked of gradual justification.' ' Expect it by faith,' he said, ' expect it as you are, expect it now. To deny one of these is to deny them all.' Dr. Adam Clarke says: ' Every penitent is exhorted to believe on the Lord Jesus, that he may receive remission of sins. He does not, he cannot, understand that the blessing thus promised is not to be received today, but at some future time. In like manner, to every believer the new heart and right spirit are offered in the present moment, that they may in that moment be received. For as the work of cleansing and renewing the heart is the work of God, His almighty power can perform it in a moment, in the twinkling of an eye. And as it is our duty to love God with all our heart, and we cannot do this until He cleanses our hearts, consequently He is ready to do it this moment; because He wills that we should in this moment love Him. Therefore we may justly say, ' Now is the accepted time; now is the day of salvation '. He who in the beginning caused light in a moment to shine out of darkness, can in a moment shine into our hearts, and give us to see the light of His glory in the face of Jesus Christ. This moment, therefore, we may be emptied of sin, filled with holiness, and become truly happy.'

Provision for our sanctification has been made as fully as for our justification, and faith must receive it. ' What is required,' says the saintly Fletcher, ' is a bold, hearty, steady venturing upon the truth of the promise, with an appropriating act.' We believe that God is able to cleanse our hearts from all sin. We believe, also, that He is willing to do this, And we know that He has promised to do it. Do we believe that having promised, He is able and willing to do it now, at this very moment, on condition of our faith? If so, the venture of faith is all that is required, which says, ' He doeth it now.' ' Though He slay me yet will I trust in Him.'

The scriptural warrant for this is very clear. ' What things soever ye desire when ye pray, believe that ye receive them and ye shall have them.' We are required to believe that we receive when we pray in order that we may have. We are not asked to believe that we have before we have, but to believe that we receive what we ask for. There are two extremes to be guarded against. Both are not far from the truth, and the more dangerous for that reason. One asks us to believe what is not true, that we have what we have not; the other leaves our faith indefinite, and asks us to believe that we shall receive at some future time. The truth is between the extremes. We are to regard God as in the act of bestowing the blessing while we pray, and to believe, not that we received it some time ago, nor that we shall receive it at some future time, but that *we receive it* just now. To believe that we *shall receive* is to make a chasm between the act of faith and the bestowment of the blessing. It is false humility which says, ' In God's appointed time I shall receive the answer to my prayer '. With Him there is no such thing as time. Centuries, years months, weeks, days are nothing to God. ' One day is with the Lord as a thousand years, and a thousand years as one day.' The conditions being fulfilled, God is as willing to grant our petition *when we pray* as ever He will be, if we are asking for spiritual blessing such as He has promised to bestow. There need be no ' ifs ', or peradventures ', or ' maybe's ', where there is a direct and specific promise. ' Ask and receive that your joy may be full.'

Faith is represented in the Scriptures as ' looking ', ' touching ', ' taking ', none of which we do gradually. We either look or we do not look, we touch or we do not touch. If a gift is offered we must either take it or we do not take it.

Faith is the hand that receives what God offers. There
is surely no presumption in doing what God directs, and
the direction is : ' When ye pray, believe that ye receive
. . . and ye shall have. . . .'   ' While they are yet
speaking I will hear.'   It is the language of true God-
inspired faith to say : —

> I take the blessing from above,
> And wonder at Thy boundless love.

Faith implies three things—knowledge, assent, and
appropriation.   We sometimes sing : —

> Faith, mighty faith, the promise sees,
> And looks to that alone.

But it sees more than that, it sees the Promiser.   It knows
that every promise is built upon four pillars, each one as
strong as the pillars of heaven—God's justice or holiness,
which will not suffer Him to deceive ; His grace and goodness, which will not suffer Him to forget ; His truth, which
will not suffer Him to change ; and His power, which
makes Him able to accomplish.   We must know God before
we can trust Him.   But knowledge is not enough in itself.
Most believers know of the power, of the love, and faithfulness of God, as well as the conditions upon which He has
promised to bless.   Many assent to the facts that God is
able and willing to bestow just now the blessing they seek,
some even go so far as to assert their conviction that if they
believe they receive it they know they shall have it, but they
fail to appropriate the promise and make it their own.
They hesitate to say, ' God does just now bestow it, *I do
receive it*', and without this all is vain.   The faith that
sanctifies says, ' God loves now and gives, I ask now and
receive '.   ' Sink or swim ', it says, ' I cast myself on this sea
of infinite love and truth.'

> In all the confidence of hope
> I claim the blessing now.

' But,' says one, ' am I to believe I receive when I feel
no change ? '   The ground of your faith must not be your

feelings, but the word of God. What we have to be sure of is that we fulfil the condition on which the promise is made. When we have done this it is our duty to believe that God answers our prayer, according to His promise. This is simple faith. We are not required to know, but to believe. When it pleases God He will give us the joyful assurance that the work is done, but in the meantime we must fix our faith upon the immutable word and keep on insisting that God is true. Faith lets God be true and every man a liar. The Divine order is, first believe, then receive, then know. Those who are waiting for feeling want to reverse this order, they want the evidnce first, the blessing next, and the faith upon which it is conditioned, last. But we cannot know that we are cleansed until the experience is an accomplished fact, and that is not possible until we believe. Feeling is not faith, nor is it salvation, nor the condition of salvation. The faith that sanctifies is ' a naked faith in a naked promise ', which means committing ourselves entirely to God and His promise, apart altogether from emotion. Feelings often mislead us, but the promise of God is sure. Trusting in the absence of all feeling may seem a risky thing, but many have done it and prove the truth of Whittier's words :—

> The foot of faith falls on the seeming void
> And finds the rock beneath.

Which is most reliable, the immutable promise of God, or our uncertain emotions? On this point, St. Peter speaks with no uncertain sound. In the first chapter of his Second Epistle he tells how, on the Mount of Transfiguration, he *heard* the voice from Heaven, he *saw* the Divine glory, and he *felt* such delightful sensations that he wanted to build three tabernacles and stay there. But he goes on to say, ' We have a more sure word of Prophecy ', something more sure than *hearing, seeing, or feeling*—the Word of God which abideth for ever. It is as though he had said our senses might have deceived us, but the Word of God is as firm as the Throne of the Eternal. We may tremble, but that Rock never will. The Blood of Christ, the veracity of God, yea, every attribute in the Diety, is pledged to the fulfilment of the promise, if we believe we receive, we *shall* have.

If the Bible is a revelation from Heaven, if there be a covenant of mercy, if there be virtue in the Blood of Christ, power in the Holy Ghost, and truth in God, *we shall have* the things we pray for, if they are what God has promised to give, and we believe we receive them when we pray.

Said a lady who was seeking the fullness of the Spirit, to her minister, ' I am expecting the Lord will give it me '. ' When will He give it you?' was the reply. After a moment's pause, she answered, timidly, ' I suppose He will give it me now '. And instead of wasting her energy in repeated petition she at once definitely accepted the price-less gift. How many are in like manner *expecting* instead of *accepting* the gift of God? It is the duty of the Christian not to pray for the accomplished outpouring of the Spirit, but to accept the Pentecostal gift. Waiting is not the connecting link between our emptiness and need, and Christ's boundless fullness and all-sufficient supply, but appropriating faith or definite accepting, irrespective of all feeling. As we believe that we receive, God bestows, and then we have what our faith claims.

Some of my readers will remember how the late Samuel Coley describes the memorable service in which he accepted Christ as a Saviour from all indwelling sin. The Rev. Thomas Collins was the preacher. His text was, ' Wilt thou be made clean? When shall it once be?' ' Unction sweeter than was wont came down as he urged the query, " When shall it once be?" Then he said, " The loving Father says, ' Now '; what do you say? " " Now," breathed audibly from pew to pew. " The Son, who gave His cleansing blood, says, ' Now '; what do you say? " At this reiteration of appeal, " Now " louder and more earnest circled me in answer. The waiting Sanctifier, the Spirit of Holiness, says, " Now "; what do you say? " When?" Twice the response, though it moved my inmost heart, had

9

passed, leaving me silent; but with the third questioning came a gush of influence irresistible. I could keep my lips no longer, but, like the rest, cried, " Now ! " What is more, and better far, my soul that blessed moment as certainly said, " Now ", as did my tongue. It was no flash of enthusiasm; it was a work of the Holy Ghost. That " Now " stirs me yet. Nor ever since that memorable time has my faith dared to procrastinate, or say anything but " Now " to all the sanctifying offers of the promise-keeping God.'

CHAPTER XXII

ADDRESS TO SEEKERS

WE do not need to have a complete grasp of the doctrine of entire sanctification in all its relations and bearings in order to enjoy the experience, but if we can have a clear and distinct view of the thing at which we aim it will help us very much to reach it as a definite point of attainment.

In one of the churches of Rome there is a beautiful painting. Those who stand in one position before it always say they see no beauty in it—that it appears like a huge tangled mass. But when the guide leads you to where the light falls properly on the picture, suddenly its wondrous beauty dawns upon you. So it is with holiness. It is only when the Holy Spirit furnishes the light that we see clearly what our privilege is. He only can reveal sin and present the remedy. When we ask humbly and earnestly for His illumination we see clearly the point we are to aim at. ' He that willeth to do His will shall know of the doctrine.'

We need not stop to settle all the points of doctrine, but *we must know what we want and seek that.*

While I take for granted that we are agreed in the main as to what entire sanctification is, let me once again mention its main characteristics. (1) It is a distinct state of grace from justification. (2) It includes the full cleansing of the soul from inbred sin, so that it becomes pure, or free from sinful inclinations and tendencies. (3) It includes the filling of the heart with all the graces and fruits of the Spirit. This means being perfected in love—filled to present capacity, and kept filled as the vessel enlarges.

David, who longed for inward purity, prayed, ' Create in me a clean heart, O God '. The Saviour prayed, 'Sanctify them through Thy truth '. The Apostle prays, ' The very God of Peace sanctify you wholly '. These are specific prayers for the blessing of entire sanctification. We must fix our attention upon this one object. This must be everything to us. As Dr. Peck says, ' For the time being the hell we would be delivered from must be the hell of inbred sin; and the heaven we would attain, the heaven of loving God alone '.

Are we convinced that this experience is attainable in this present life?

A firm conviction on this point goes far towards our realizing it. Some believe that such a state may be approximated, but never reached. But what man will strive long for what he believes to be impossible? ' We are saved by hope.' Confidence that we shall succeed is essential to sustain us in the pursuit of the experience we have in view. Does not the Bible command us to be holy? If the experience is not attainable, God requires what is impossible. God will surely give that which He commandeth.

And is this experience not expressly promised in the Scriptures? What could be clearer than such a statement as ' Then will I sprinkle clean water upon you, and ye shall be clean: from all your filthiness and from all your idols will I cleanse you ' (Ezekiel xxxvi. 25). Other promises might be quoted, but in the case of such a direct utterance they are not necessary. Repeated and varied statements may heighten the certainty that the exact idea is apprehended, but one, ' Thus saith the Lord ', is sufficient to establish any truth. ' If we deny the possibility of being free from sin in this world,' says St. Augustine, ' we violate man's free will who voluntarily desires it, and God's power who offers to accomplish it.'

Would inspired men have made this the subject of definite, fervent and earnest prayer if they had not believed their prayers could be answered? Was not the Son of God manifested ' to destroy the works of the Devil ', and is it not distinctly stated that ' the Blood of Jesus Christ His Son cleanseth us from all sin '? If these are ' the true sayings of God ',

Rejoice in hope, rejoice with me,
We shall from all our sin be free.

Receiving this truth into our minds, let us resolve *that we will seek the experience at once, that we shall give God no rest until we hear Him speak the second time, 'Be clean '.* None but those who have a settled, uncompromising and unconquerable purpose will succeed. It will require invincible resolution not to hesitate when the knife is put to the heart to amputate its idols. A feeble resolution will soon be overcome, and many fail for want of this strength of purpose. Is there one whom difficulties dishearten, who bends to the storm? He will do but little. Is there one who will conquer? That kind of man always succeeds. God yields to a thoroughly determined soul, just as difficulties do. The violent take the Kingdom of Heaven by force. Intensity of spirit, importunity, and perseverance in prayer will surely prevail. Our great need is more desire. ' Desires,' says an old writer, ' are the sails of the mind.' When our desire is deep, intense, burning enough to make us willing to sacrifice every idol, to put away all evil, not to shrink when God demands what is dear as a right hand or precious as a right eye, we shall soon hear a voice from the Throne saying, ' Be it unto thee even as thou wilt '.

Instead of frittering away our time in contemplation, let us at once resolutely make up our minds that we will have the blessing now. Our effort will soon grow feeble, and our vehement desire cool down, unless we adhere to the idea of present blessing. This determination is all-important and needs to be emphasized repeatedly. Payson's dying regret was that he had only lived a few months in Beulah Land when he might have lived there thirty years. ' Many are not in the enjoyment of holiness simply because they have never reached a point at which they have said, " I must have the blessing now ". This remark by Mrs. Palmer led a minister some years ago to see the cause of his failure. He went immediately to his study, locked the door, and falling upon his knees determined he would never leave the room until he had been cleansed from all sin. Since that day he has borne constant witness to the power of Christ to save to the uttermost. We must put a ' now ' into our prayers. Unless we do this we pray in vain.

Does it seem too great a thing that in a moment our sinful nature can be purified, that all the evil within can be uprooted, and our whole being filled with light and love and power. Our answer is, ' Is anything too hard for the Lord?' *It is God's work, and what He undertakes He will accomplish.* He graciously condescends to assure us of His ability to save us to the uttermost. ' Wherefore He is able, also, to save them to the uttermost that come unto God by Him, seeing He ever liveth to make intercession for them ' (Heb. vii. 25). Amongst the many mighty words of Scripture there are few, if any, so full and grand as this word ' uttermost '. It is easy to see that it is composed of two words; *utter,* and *most; utter* means total, complete, entire, perfect; *most* means the utmost extent, the highest degree, the farthest point. Put the two words together, and we learn that Christ is able to save perfectly, to the uttermost extent of our need.

But no English words can express completely the fullness of meaning contained in the original word. Translators have all been puzzled with it, and in consequence we find it translated very differently by various authorities. Dr. Mahan gives the literal translation as ' all perfection '. In the Dutch Bible it is rendered ' perfectly '; in the German, ' for ever '; in the Catholic, ' eternally ', and by Dr. Stier, ' most completely '. Dean Alford says, ' Some take this for time, for ever; but this is not the use of the word. *Completeness* is the idea.' Perhaps Dr. Clarke is nearest the mark when he says, ' The original word seems to combine the two ideas of continuity and utmost completeness; hence Jesus is able to save forever to the utmost '. This is not unlike Luther's translation, ' Always, under all circumstances, and at all times, all that come to God by Him.' What can this assurance mean if God is not willing to save to the extent indicated by this word? What benefit would it be to tell the Church that He had power to do this, if there were not implied an intention to do for us what He is able to do, and what we all need to have done?

But that all doubt may be removed from our minds as to the Divine ability to save with this all-comprehensive completeness (and ability here is so necessarily connected with willingness, that the one indisputably implies the other), St. Paul concludes his remarkable prayer for the Ephesian Christians by asserting that God ' is able to do exceeding abundantly, above all our asking and thinking.' Read through that prayer, as recorded in Ephesians iii. 14-19. It would surely seem that neither language nor thought could grasp any greater wealth of blessing. But no; God's power to bless must not be confined to what even Paul can ask and think. So he concludes with a wondrous doxology, that shall for ever forbid any attempt to limit our conceptions of the exceeding greatness of the power of Christ to save. ' Now unto Him that is able to do exceeding abundantly, above all that we ask or think, according to the power that worketh in us; unto Him be glory in the Church by Christ Jesus throughout all ages, world without end. Amen.' How inspiring to know that God is able to do all we ask. But St. Paul adds, ' or think '. Thought can go far beyond language, but even all our thinking does not come up to the measure of God's power and bountifulness, as expressed in this passage. Dr. Clarke says the idea is ' superabundantly—above the greatest abundance '. No words can express what God is able and willing to do for the soul that commits itself fully to Him. But how we have limited the Holy One of Israel. We have done as Martha and her sister Mary did when they came to Jesus in their trouble about their departed brother. The great mistake they made was to limit the Master's power. First, they limited Him as to *place*—' Lord, if Thou hadst been *here* '. Then they limited Him as to *time*. He had been ' buried four days '. And lastly they limited Him as to *degree*. They believed that He would be raised at the last day, but they did not believe that Jesus could do it *now*. Do not let us fall into this same error. Let us think less of the weakness of our broken-down humanity, and more of 'the exceeding greatness of His power to usward who believe'. Surely our faith need not stagger when the God who created the universe and who upholds it by the word of His power undertakes to immediately cleanse our hearts from inbred sin by the putting forth of His omnipotent power. Did not our Lord while on earth make men perfectly whole? His healing work on the body was immediate and complete. That was a type of His work on the soul. When we learn to estimate aright the exceeding riches of His grace we shall not hesitate to say : —

> I, even I, shall see His face ;
> I shall be holy here.

To this confidence that God is able and willing to cleanse our souls from all sin now, there needs to be added one thing more—a Divine evidence and conviction that He *doeth* it. That even now, as I venture myself upon Him, the very God of Peace sanctifies me wholly, and Christ's most precious blood cleanses me from all sin. If our consecration be real and thorough, and we are willing to forsake all, to live a life of self-surrender, of self-nothingness, to lose ourselves in God, appropriating faith is the one thing lacking. We must determine that we will believe, come what will. 'Likewise, reckon ye also yourselves to be dead indeed unto sin, but alive unto God through Jesus Christ our Lord.' The word 'reckon' is only another word for faith. We obtain full salvation by reckoning or believing at God's bidding that we are 'dead indeed unto sin'. 'As when you reckon with your creditor or with your host,' says Mr. Fletcher, 'and as when you have paid all, you reckon yourself free, so now reckon with God. Jesus has paid all, and He hath paid for thee—hath purchased thy pardon and holiness. Therefore, it is now God's command, "Reckon thyself dead unto sin, and thou art alive unto God from this hour"'. The very command is in itself a pledge that in the moment of our faith God will work in us what He bids us believe. Our duty is just to obey, not to question. God will make the reckoning good, or His word is a deception.

It may be in direct contradiction to all our past and present experience to say, ' I am dead to sin ; henceforth I live only for God ', but God commands it and we must not hesitate. We cannot be wrong in obeying the command and venturing to believe or reckon that God does now, by the power of His spirit, fulfil in us the work of faith with power. It is not more prayer that is needed. The time has come when prayer must give place to faith. The command now is not ' ask ', but ' take '. Have you made room for Christ by a thorough consecration to Him? If so, reckon He does come to His temple, that He does fully possess you, and because He fills you with His life you are now ' dead unto sin and alive unto God '. ' O, begin, begin to reckon now ; fear not, believe, believe, believe, and continue to believe every moment. So shalt thou continue free, for it is retained, as it is received, by faith alone.'

> 'Tis done, Thou dost this moment save,
>   With full salvation bless ;
> Redemption through Thy blood I have,
>   And spotless love and peace.

Our chapter on this subject would not be complete if mention were not made of the fact that it is possible to seek the blessing of holiness from unworthy motives. Murray M'Cheyne saw the peril of seeking a higher experience for notoriety—to establish a reputation for sanctity—he mentions how he felt the necessity of watching against this. Of all unholy things there is surely nothing more loathsome in the sight of God than a desire to be reputed saintly for the credit of the thing. A second danger is the desire for prominence among those who are eminently useful. Some seek a higher life in the hope of becoming the Moodys and Spurgeons of their day and generation. They seek fame and popularity to augment their own importance. Others have in view the delicious ecstasy which it will bring. Their desire is to be happy—the exhilaration, the rapture of the life is the object of their quest. They seek the gift, not the Giver. These are all subtle forms of self-seeking. The desire for a fuller life must rise from a loftier motive. It must centre in God. He must be sought for His own worthiness. The attraction must be the incomparable beauty of His character, not any mere gift at His disposal. To glorify Him must be our aim, perfect identity of interest with Christ, not personal enjoyment or reputation. Thus saith the Lord God, ' I do not this for your sakes, O House of Israel, but for My Holy Name's sake ' (Ezekiel xxxvi. 22).

CHAPTER XXIII

HOW TO RETAIN THE BLESSING

THERE is no step in Christian life that God and man do not take together. From beginning to end in the work of salvation there must be both Divine and human action. The words preserve and persevere are so much alike that the one can be spelt from the other. If we are to be preserved we must persevere. It is true that salvation in one sense is all of God, but it is also true that the gifts and graces of the spirit are only ours when certain conditions are complied with. Peter declares that in Christian life ' we are kept by the power of God ', but St. James teaches that the godly man must ' keep *himself* unspotted from the world '. The Bible does not contradict itself. To careful readers it explains itself, and the explanation is, that while grace is altogether the gift of God we ourselves have an important part to play. We are to ' work out ' the salvation which God works within. To grow in grace we must avail ourselves of the means of grace. Christ's promise to keep us involves the condition that we do not go needlessly into the way of temptation. We are only on covenant ground when we keep within the borders of the land of strict obedience to the Divine will. If we leave this prescribed territory, presuming that God will deliver us, we shall find ourselves sadly mistaken. We are to keep ourselves in the love of God. This is true of entire sanctification as it is of any other state of grace. A few suggestions as to how we may do this may help save some from spiritual downfall.

I. WE MUST WALK IN THE LIGHT

Our consecration must keep pace with the ever-widening circle of illumination. As we rise higher in Christian life we shall have clearer vision, quickened sensibilities, and increasingly clear perception of what the will of God is. This means that we shall discover that many a course we had pursued, or a state of mind we had indulged, which we did not understand at the time to be wrong or questionable, will have to be rectified. Clearer apprehensions of truth resulting from enlightenment and cultivation of conscience will necessarily lead to scrutiny of motive, temper, speech and conduct. There is no need that we should be condemned when we are made aware of evils which we had never known or suspected; but when more accurate perceptions of duty and danger are granted, we must be immediately obedient to the heavenly vision. Those who walk with God will see as they look back on the path they have trodden all sorts of ' doubtful ' and ' inexpedient ' abandonments, which with senses not ' exercised to discern between good and evil ' were once indulged in without condemnation or self-reproach. Not until the wrong or the hindrance was seen was it forsaken, but when the light came they followed it. There is safety in no other course. The obedience of those who walk with God will often be tested by new revelations of His will.

The primary act of consecration need not be repeated but it must be daily reorganized and confirmed. ' It is a constant, an uninterrupted and unending consecration, a point carried on into an endless line.' It must continue complete, corresponding with increasing light, through all our life. Nearly all who once experienced entire sanctification, and have lost the blessing, are conscious of having refused obedience to some distinct command which came into their life and from which they shrank. Some duty was borne upon them, and they knew it to be of God, but they hesitated to obey. When they left the narrow track of implicit obedience to the leadings of the Spirit, fellowship with God ceased, and the sense of the abiding of the Comforter was gone. Since then a shadow has been over their lives, they have made no progress, and have lacked both power and joy. Nor will they ever find the blessing again until they go back to the place where they dropped the thread of obedience, and perform the thing which God then demanded. From beginning to end, the Bible rings out with one long demand for uncompromising obedience.

> To keep thy conscience sensitive,
> No inward motion miss;
> But go where grace entices thee,
> Perfection lies in this.

II. WE MUST KEEP A LIFE OF SIMPLE TRUST

The life we live in the flesh must be by the faith of the Son of God. The same faith by which we received and relied upon the Lord Jesus as our Saviour is that by which we abide in Him. That act was not performed once for all. It needs to be perpetually renewed. We retain the blessing of holiness by the constant repetition of the faith by which we received it. We must believe moment by moment that the blood of Jesus Christ cleanses us from all sin. On the first approach of temptation, doubt, or perplexity, it is well to define our position immediately; that is, to declare in our hearts in spite of all the mutiny of doubt, reason, or sense, that the blood of Jesus does now cleanse from all sin. We must hold on there by simple faith, insisting that God is true, until the trial is over.

The Holy Spirit is an abiding guest in the heart of every sanctified Christian, but times will come when the sense of His Presence will be dulled. Our spiritual sky will be darkened. It will seem as though every emotion had subsided, and to an inexperienced soul the absence of desire, joy, and peace, will cause alarm. The temptation will come that perhaps you have fallen and grieved away the Spirit of God. But do not be disturbed. Such experiences are permitted for our chastening and strengthening, and that Christ may be everything to us, rather than any of His gifts. When such experiences occur those who have learned to live the life of faith hang on to the unchangeable promise like a drowning man to a lifebuoy, and say, ' I will trust and not be afraid '. Sooner or later God is sure to reveal

Himself again to such a soul, with more glorious manifestations of His love than ever before, to reward faithful clinging to the naked word. God is still true, though for brief periods we may have no evidence of His presence in our feelings.

No greater mistake can be made than to measure our piety by our emotions. As the etymology of the word indicates, emotion is always moving, waxing and waning continually. Our feelings are changeable as the wind and the tides, and fickle as April weather. Health, education, natural temperament, and much else apart altogether from religion, combine to modify them. But faith, while it rests upon the promise, knows no change. 'The Lord has taught me,' says Lady Maxwell, 'that it is by faith and not joy I must live.' The holy Fénelon says, 'Naked faith alone is a sure guard against illusion'. We must cease to consider how we feel, and build upon the immovable rock of God's Word and faithfulness. We may tremble, but the Rock of Ages never does. None of our changeable moods can affect or alter the fact that the blood of Jesus cleanses from all sin. We must meet every suggestion of doubt by the decisive answer that God is faithful and must do as He has said. Faith is 'an affirmation and an act, which bids eternal truth be present fact'.

III. WE MUST TAKE TIME FOR PRAYERFUL MEDITATION OF THE WORD OF GOD

Richard Watson says, 'The Word of God is the food of faith'. This is true especially of the state of full trust in Christ; it is rooted in the soil of the Divine Word. We must take time to read, mark and inwardly digest spiritual truth, if we would promote spiritual growth and strengthen all the elements of spiritual life. The best devotional literature is only truly helpful so far as it has its roots in 'the true sayings of God'. Hasty snatches of this Heavenly manna are not without benefit, but if we would 'dwell on high places' we must make the Bible our chief Book.

The higher life takes root only in a deeper knowledge of God's Word. Eating the Word is like Jonathan's honey, the instrument of enlightenment. It is astonishing what new beauties are unfolded, what new wonders are discovered, what strength and comfort are derived, when we obey the command to Ezekiel, ' Son of Man, eat the roll '.

Dr. Horace Bushnell voiced the experience of many when he said, ' My experience is that the Bible is dull when I am dull. When I am really alive and set in upon the text with a tidal pressure of living affinities, it opens, it multiplies discoveries and reveals depths even faster than I can note them. The worldly spirit shuts the Bible; the Spirit of God makes it a fire, flaming out all meanings and glorious truths.' There is no more certain sign of ill-health in spiritual as in physical life than to have no appetite for our food. Those are already on the path to spiritual declension who have ceased to feed regularly upon the Word of God. ' Man shall not live by bread alone, but by every word that proceedeth out of the mouth of God.' To cultivate the devotional spirit, to strengthen conviction, and to draw strength and life from the Fountain of Life in God, there is nothing more essential than a constant and prayerful study of the Holy Scriptures. It is not the careless or listless reading of the Book, but its entrance into the soul, that produces spiritual illumination and strength. ' The entrance of Thy Word giveth light.'

IV. WE MUST ENGAGE ACTIVELY IN CHRISTIAN WORK

An old writer has said, ' We must combine Bible diet with Bible duty, or we shall make no progress '. Blessing is given as a motive to labour. We must pass on the blessing we have received or we shall soon have nothing to pass on. There is truth in the saying that ' a Christian is like a live coal, he must set others on fire or he will go out himself ', Whittier sings : —

> Heaven's gate is closed to him who comes alone,
> Save thou a soul, so shalt thou save thine own.

This is not all truth, but there is a great truth in it; there can be no spiritual life or health apart from work for God and souls. The reflex influence of Christian work upon a man himself is scarcely less important and valuable than the direct influence upon unsaved souls. In it lies the secret of growth and joy. It is the same in grace as in Nature; standing water becomes stagnant, a man who takes no exercise becomes an invalid, the limb that is not used withers and shrivels, it is the still pond, not the running stream, that freezes. We can only save ourselves by trying to save others. We see with clearer eyes in trying to make others see. We lift our burdens more easily by helping others to bear their burdens. Unselfish toil for others always brings its own reward. God's law is *use* or *lose*. There is nothing good which is not lessened, and lost at last, by not using. In sending us to work God not only has the salvation of the lost at heart, but the best good of the Christian. 'Mother,' said a bright little girl of ten, who had just found the Saviour, 'shall I run over the way and tell the old shoemaker that Jesus has pardoned all my sins?' 'It would do him no good, my dear, he is an infidel and does not believe in these things,' said the mother. 'But it would do me good to tell him,' said the child. And she was right. Selfishness and self-absorption swell our worst self, and shrink and shrivel our better nature, but interest in and effort for the benefit and salvation of others feed and develop that other and nobler self. That is a beautiful myth that represents birds as at first created without wings. They could sing, but they could not fly. Then God gave them wings and told them to fly. The birds at first complained that they were heavy, but they soon found that the burden they complained of was the means by which they could soar up to heights of cloudless day. Our duties are our wings. When we first assume them they seem like burdens, but cheerfully borne they become less and less heavy, and eventually become the wings by which we mount higher and higher into the life of God.

V. We must never be satisfied with present attainments

As we have already explained there is childhood in sanctification. Purity of heart is but the preparation for advancement in knowledge, love and holiness. There is no finality in this life of faith and charity. There are ever deeper depths to be fathomed and higher heights to be climbed. It is always from grace to grace, from strength to strength and from glory to glory. Growth is the great law of life in the spiritual as in the animal and vegetable kingdoms. By various figures and illustrations the Gospel represents growth as the Christian's privilege and duty. Now we have the leaven that works until the whole lump is leavened. Then we have the corn, with the blade first, then the ear, and the full corn at last. There are babes in Christian life and there are those with a robust, manly, well-developed Christian character.

Character is formed gradually. It has been well described as ' consolidated habits '. Acts often repeated become habits. But action is the outcome of condition. Holiness deals with the inner condition, it fills the soul with love, joy and peace. The result is right conduct, and right conduct has permanent effect upon the character. We shall develop gradually a full-orbed Christian character if we maintain day by day that purity of heart of which right conduct is the practical outcome. It is not enough that ' we stand fast in the liberty wherewith God has made us free. We must add to our faith virtue; and to virtue knowledge; and to knowledge temperance; and to temperance patience; and to patience godliness; and to godliness brotherly kindness; and to brotherly kindness charity.'

If we would grow in grace we must be always aiming at something above and beyond us. ' A pupil from whom nothing is ever demanded which he cannot do, never does all he can '. Even St. Paul had not reached his ideal which he described as ' the mark ', the ' high calling ', ' that

10

for which I am apprehended ', but he was determined to press on until he realized the purpose of his calling. The last word is never said, the last effort is never made; to retain entire sanctification we must be ever ' reaching forth unto those things which are before '. We shall lose the grace we have unless we seek for more. Our motto must always be forward, onward, upward.

Beyond each hill-top others rise, like ladder-rungs, to loftier skies.
Each halt is but a breathing-space for . . . fresher pace,
    Till who dare say, 'ere night descend,
    ' There can be such a thing as end '?

CHAPTER XXIV

THE ARBITER OF THE HEART.

THE maintenance of a good conscience towards God from day to day is essential to the life of faith. True spirituality cannot exist unless accompanied by scrupulous conscientiousness, the purpose to do right at any cost. Archbishop Temple has truly said, ' It is always a duty to obey conscience; it is never a duty to disobey '. Conscience requires that we mean well, and do our best. It requires not only that we follow all the light we have, but all that we can obtain, and that we do this gladly. Conscience claims regency in everything that a man should aim to do or to be. ' The word *ought* is the sovereign of all vocabularies.'

But conscience guarantees only good intentions. Apart from knowledge and sound judgement, even those who are most conscientious may do immense mischief under the impression that they are doing the will of God. In some, conscience develops singular incongruities. Men are often very scrupulous in certain things, and very lax in other things. Frederick Robertson emphasizes the fact that scrupulosity about details often slides into laxity about the eternal laws of right and wrong. The brigands of Italy would go to the confessional most obediently before starting on an adventure of robbery and murder.

The Rev. John Newton, the author of some of the most valuable hymns in the English language, was once, as is well known, a slave-trader on the coast of Africa. After his conversion his moral stupor was such that he saw no necessity for abandoning his diabolical trade. On his last voyage to the African coast for cargo, he said, he ' experienced sweeter and more frequent hours of Divine communion than he had ever known before '. He wrote again of this infamous occupation : ' No other employment affords greater advantages for promoting the life of God in the soul, especially to one who has command of a ship.' This is the testimony of a slave-dealer. Yet the piety of John Newton at the time was scarcely less questionable than that of St. Paul. His moral sense had not been educated to see the exceptional depravity of the course he was pursuing.

The Bible itself speaks of conscience as seared, blunted, and blinded. We have Scriptural warrant for saying that the conscience may be seared as with a hot iron. In Newton's case it was drugged, so as to give out delirious judgement. He had written several of the hymns for Christian worship which the Church sings to-day before he found out the depth of the moral abyss in which his moral nature was rotting. But when the awakening did come, he vaulted from the extreme of moral stupor to the extreme of moral hysteria. From the conviction that nothing was sin, his moral sense came to the conviction that everything was sin. For a time he could scarcely be persuaded to converse on other than religious topics, lest he should incur the guilt of ' idle words '.

Is there any tyranny worse than that of an unenlightened conscience? Of all our ignorances and infirmities, none are more disastrous to Christian character than to fall into bondage to the ascetic scruples and tyrannical prohibitions of a conscience not healthfully instructed and mollified by good sense. It is reported that Oberlin once fell on his knees in a remorseful prayer, because he had despatched a letter in which he had neglected to cross the t's and dot the i's accurately. We may smile at his folly, but there are few Christians who cannot recall vagaries quite as foolish in their own lives, during temporary subjection to an austere conscience.

It is because of such possibilities of perversion and contortion that the human conscience is not always a safe and infallible guide. The moral sense in man is not designed to stand alone in the conduct of life and the building of character. God has provided the Christian with another arbiter to decide between good and evil, which is perfectly competent and reliable. ' Let the peace of God,' says the apostle, ' *rule* in your hearts ' (Col. iii. 15). Much of the force of the expression is lost by the use of the colourless word ' *rule* ', which is translated ' arbitrate ' in the margin of the Revised Version.

' It is evident,' says an eminent Bible exegete, ' that St. Paul intended something peculiar by the use of the Greek word " arbitrate ", found nowhere else in the Holy Scriptures, and styled " a remarkable word " by Bengel.' ' Wherever,' says Bishop Lightfoot, ' there is a conflict of motives, or impulses, or reasons, the peace of God must step in and decide which is to prevail.' Dr. Maclaren explains that ' the figure contained in the word translated *rule* is that of the umpire or arbitrator at the games, who, looking down on the arena, watches that the combatants strive lawfully, and adjudges the prize '.

This arbiter is not peace *with* God, but the peace *of* God, the fathomless ocean of Christ's peace, which He has left as a legacy to His people. ' My peace I give unto you.' It is that deep repose of spirit which we receive when we enthrone the God of peace as the Lord of our hearts and lives. When this peace becomes the paramount consideration, everything that disturbs that profound rest of the soul will be instinctively avoided, and every act that would weave the thinnest veil between us and the face of our adorable Saviour, we shall instantly shrink from. A man who is exploring an old well lowers a candle before him, knowing that where that can live, he can live. If the light goes out, he knows that it is not safe to go farther. The peace of God is the Christian's test-flame. Anything that in the slightest degree disturbs it should be instantly discarded, otherwise the storm has begun which will wreck the fair beauty and happiness of the soul.

The question of worldly amusements has been before the court of conscience for centuries, but no final decision has been reached. Before this arbiter, which the Gospel has called to the judgement-seat of the soul, the matter is quickly settled. What we cannot do quietly we cannot do safely. Whatever mars our tranquillity or interferes with our inward repose, is detrimental to spiritual life. If we find that a given course of action tends to break our peace, we may be certain that there is poison in the draught, which, as in the old stories, has been detected by the shivered cup, and we should not drink any more. Conscience may discern no evil, but the peace of God is a more delicate instrument, dealing with questions too subtle for conscience to answer, and operating in a higher sphere.

The peace of God will approve of nothing into which Christ cannot be introduced and assigned the seat of honour. It should be to us what the barometer is to the sailor, and if it sinks, let us take warning. Whenever we find it in peril, we must retrace our steps. In all matters of doubt, when contending impulses and reasons distract, and seem to pull in opposite directions, our safety is to ' let the peace of God ' decide which is to prevail. Under His watchful rule the soul settles down into resolute and calm obedience to the law of Christ. The hearts and lives of men are made troubled, not by circumstances, but by themselves. We are restless because our wills are not in harmony with the will of God.

' A calm and heavenly frame ' is only possible to those who let the peace of God have its way in their hearts. That stillness of the spirit is so sensitive, that it shrinks immediately in the presence of an evil thing. Our peace is gone immediately when we allow what it forbids. Happy are those who have enthroned the peace of God as the arbiter of their hearts! We share with Christ then, not only the peace that He gives, but ' the peace which lay like a great calm on the sea, on His own deep heart '.

> The halcyon rest within,
> Calming the storms of dread and sin.

CHAPTER XXV

TESTIMONY

THE Rev. John Fletcher once said to Mrs. Hester Ann Rogers, ' Come, my sister, we will covenant together to spread the sacred flame, and testify before men and angels " the blood of Jesus Christ cleanseth us from all sin ".' With flowing tears Mrs. Rogers replied, ' In the strength of Jesus I will '; and she did, until she went ' sweeping through the gates, washed in the blood of the Lamb '. It seems to have been the custom among early Methodists to make humble, prudent, but frank acknowledgement of the work of entire sanctification, when it was wrought in their souls by the power of the Holy Ghost. We give a few testimonies which come first to hand :—

' The Lord for whom I waited came suddenly to the temple of my heart, and I had an immediate evidence that this was the blessing I had for some time been seeking.'

' No sooner had I uttered the words " I shall have the blessing now " than refining fire went through my heart, illuminating my soul, scattered its life through every part, and sanctified the whole. I then received the full witness of the Spirit that the blood of Jesus had cleansed me from all sin.'

' My heart was softened, and warmed, and filled; my prayer was turned into praises, and I could do nothing but shout, " Glory be to God ". Whether I hold or not, I am sure that God took full possession of my heart on the 14th of July.'

These are but samples of the numerous testimonies which have been handed down to us in the biographies of those who are held up before us as ' epistles ' to be ' read and known of all men '.

At first Mr. Wesley advised that great caution should be exercised in making definite confession of heart purity, but as the doctrine and experience became more generally known and appreciated, he changed his attitude, and constantly urged the duty to confess it upon ministers and people. Writing to John King, one of his preachers, in 1787, he said, ' It requires a great deal of watchfulness to retain the perfect love of God; and one great means of retaining it is, frankly to declare what God has given you, and earnestly to exhort all the believers you meet to follow after full salvation.' It was soon found that this testimony humbly and truthfully given moved the hearts of others as nothing else could do. Those who heard it were stimulated to seek the same grace, and a general revival followed. ' With the heart man believeth unto righteousness, and with the mouth confession is made unto salvation.'

The testimony of the cleansed leper will do more to recommend the physician than the most persuasive and cogent arguments. We might advertise a remedy for cancer, but who would believe in our remedy unless we could point to some we had cured? St. Paul recognized experience to be one of the chief elements of Evangelical power. Writing to Philemon, he said, ' That the communication of thy faith may become effectual by the acknowledging of every good thing which is in you in Christ Jesus.' Though he was the master logician, on occasions when life and liberty were at stake, he did not attempt any elaborate argument to justify his action, but told the story of his conversion. Three times his commission was renewed, and each time he was reminded that he was chosen not so much to preach as to testify. St. John often left the advocate's stand and entered the witness-box, as is seen from the frequent occurrence of the words ' We know ', so characteristic of his Epistles. He believed that man might be saved from all sin and *know* it, so as to be able to testify, as he did, ' The Blood of Jesus cleanseth *us* from all sin '.

The great need of our times is a witnessing Church and ministry. ' Ye are My witnesses, saith the Lord.' Not that we would recommend loud professions as to attainment. Instead of professing anything, let us confess Christ as a Saviour from all sin, if we have proved Him to be such.

This will make Him and what He is to us prominent as contrasted with some attainment which might call attention to ourselves. If by humbly declaring how great things God hath done for us we can encourage some trembling and fainting soul, and kindle desire after like precious blessing, it would be cowardice or false prudence not to do it with humility. For this reason the writer ventures once again to relate how he was led into the experience which he has, in these pages, been attempting to describe.

My conversion was so clear and satisfactory that I could never doubt its reality. Need I say it was an eventful day in my history when I first realized God's pardoning mercy, and received the assurance of His favour? The beginnings of this life of loyalty and love I shall never forget. It seems but yesterday, though many years have now passed since the love of God was shed abroad in my heart, and I was reconciled to God, who loved me, even me. It was a change as from death unto life. A new fountain of joys was at once opened in my heart, so exceedingly precious and sweet as to utterly extinguish all desire for that which I had called pleasure before. All my fears of death, judgement, and hell were fully swept away, and I could do nothing but praise God continually. My tastes, desires, and impulses were all changed; 'all things became new'. I was truly a new creature, and seemed to be in a new world.

With such experiences is it any wonder I imagined the work of moral renovation was perfected, that sin was not only forgiven, but fully expelled from my soul? But soon I discovered my mistake. My highly-wrought emotions subsided, and petty annoyances of life chafed, the temptations of the devil assailed; and then I found out, as pride, envy, unbelief, self-will, and other forms of heart-sin stirred within me, that much needed to be done before I could be 'meet for the inheritance of the saints in light'. The 'old man' was bound, but not cast out; the disease was modified, but not eradicated; sin was suspended, but not fully destroyed. True, sin was stunned and deadened, and held in check by grace; its power was broken, but its pollution continued. It did not reign, but it existed, making its presence felt in a constant 'bent to sinning', and at times a painful sense of duality contrasting most strikingly with the sweet feeling of oneness with Christ I now experience. There were foes within as well as without; some of the Canaanites remained, and were thorns in my side and pricks in my eyes; the flesh and spirit were in a state of antagonism, which I saw to be manifestly only a temporary position—one or the other must eventually conquer; the light was mingled with darkness, and love with its opposites.

How many headaches and heartaches I had in struggling with my bosom foes, no language can describe. All the time I was enjoying sweet fellowship with Christ, was blessedly conscious of acceptance in Him, was an earnest worker in the Lord's vineyard, and would rather have died than wilfully sinned against Him. But though I never was a backslider in the ordinary sense, my Christian life was unsatisfactory, at least to myself. There was much of vacillation about it, sinning and repenting, advancing and retrograding, swinging like a pendulum between God and the world. My experience was full of fits and starts, changeable and uneven. I was conscious also of a mighty want; there seemed a vacuum in my nature which grace had not filled, a strange sense of need, which I cannot describe, but which all who love the Lord Jesus with less than perfect love will understand. My religion moreover was full of action, but I saw little result from my efforts. I fear now that to furnish subject-food for self-worship was the great end in much that I did, and not the glory of Jesus.

For three years this half-and-half sort of life continued, when I was so dissatisfied that I felt unless I had something better I could not go on any longer. Reading Methodist biographies about this time stirred my heart, and filled me with hope for better things. I thought what God had done for others He could do for me; and an inexpressible longing possessed me to enjoy the fullness of which they spoke. I began at once to seek it, determined to give God no rest until I was sanctified wholly. The more earnestly I sought the worse I seemed to become. What a view I had of the sinfulness of my own heart! I saw what a charnel-house it was—a depth of depravity there which would at once have utterly paralysed my faith, and extinguished my hope. I then apprehended the goodness of God in not revealing to me my need of cleansing when I sought forgiveness. It was enough that I should realize my guilt and exposure to the pangs of the second death when I came to God at first. Had I then seen my own heart sin as I saw it afterwards, I believe I should have despaired in view of the difficulties; so God's revelation of my need was tempered in mercy until I had strength enough to receive it. It was in my case very similar to that of Professor Upham : ' the remains of every form of internal opposition to God appeared to be centred in one point—selfishness! ' I had once prayed to be saved from hell, but prayer to be saved from *myself* now was immeasurably more fervent. How I struggled and wrestled for the victory I shall never be able to tell, but sin and self die hard.

From experiences I had read and listened to I imagined it would be all gladness entering into this rest, but I found it a different process. The way was through the garden and by the cross; I had to learn the hard lesson that every victory is gained by surrender, and that the place of life is the place of death. I saw it all clearly enough, that before there could be a full and glorious resurrection to spiritual life and blessedness, there must first be a complete death of self—my hands must be empty if I would grasp a whole Christ. Again and again I searched my heart, and surrendered, praying all the while that any idol might be uncovered of which I was unconscious, that the Holy Spirit would make demand after demand until self were exhausted. Perhaps my reputation was the last thing laid on the altar. How concerned I used to be for the good opinion of my fellow mortals, instead of seeking the honour that comes from God only! But I see now that I never had any reputation until I gave it to God. Blessed paradox, ' He that loseth his life for My sake shall save it ', and in all other matters this is equally true. Acting upon the advice of one deeply experienced in Divine things, I wrote upon paper the several items included as well as the obligations assumed in the complete consecration of myself to God. I did this to secure definiteness of surrender.

At last I felt sure, so far as I knew it (and we are not responsible for what we do not know), that upon all I had I could honestly inscribe ' Sacred to Jesus '. The language of my soul was ' None of self, and all of Thee '. But still the Lord tarried. Why did He not come and fill His Temple? I afterwards saw that it was because I did not receive Him by simple faith. In consecration we give all, by faith we take all, and the one is as essential as the other. I had received justification by faith, but was seeking sanctification by works. What strugglings and wrestlings and tears I might have been saved, had I known the simple way of faith then as I do now; but I had no one to help me.

Some months passed, during which I was at times almost in a state of despair; but my extremity was God's opportunity. At this very juncture, when I felt I must die unless I received the grace, an Evangelist came to our town, and proclaimed ' full salvation ' to be a present duty and privilege. There was no disputing his teaching; if by faith, it must be a present experience. Faith cannot be otherwise than an instantaneous operation. It was like a revelation from heaven to me, and I rejoiced in hope, though not in actual possession of the fullness, during his visit. Some friends entered into rest before he left, but, greatly to my disappointment, I did not. Instead of receiving Christ, as my Saviour to the uttermost in the absence of all feeling, I waited for some wondrous emotion, some great exaltation of soul. In fact, I was seeking the experience of another friend, who had been prostrated under the weight of glory which fell upon him as he wrestled for the blessing. How many seekers make this same mistake! They forget that in all God's works is beautiful variety, and in the spiritual world this is as true as in the natural world. He scarcely ever deals with two persons alike. I had set the Lord a plan to work by, and was disappointed. Instead of in the earthquake, God spoke to me in the 'still small voice'. I saw my blunder afterwards, and was willing to be blessed in God's own way, with or without emotion. It was then— oh, glory to His Name!—He spoke to me the second time, 'Be clean'.

The circumstances were as follows:—A few friends who had received 'full salvation' during the Evangelist's visit decided to meet together week by week, to encourage each other in the way, and assist those who might be seeking the experience. It was at the first meeting where the Lord met me. After listening to their experiences I could bear no longer, but asked them to begin at once to pray that I might enter in. I fell upon my knees, with the determination not to rise again until my request was granted. The passage, 'If we walk in the light, as He is in the light, we have fellowship one with another, and the blood of Jesus Christ His Son cleanseth us from all sin', was instantly applied to my heart, and with such power as I had never felt before. What a fullness of meaning I saw in the words! Was I walking in the light? Truthfully I could answer, 'Yes, Lord; so far as I know Thy will I am doing it, and will do it, by Thy grace helping me'. I then saw that the passage was not so much a promise as a plain declaration. If I walked in the light, the full cleansing from sin was my heritage, and all I had to do was to immediately claim it. Without a moment's hesitation I did so, and cried out at the top of my voice, 'I claim the blessing now'. My friends then began to sing—

> 'Tis done! Thou dost this moment save,
>   With full salvation bless;
> Redemption through Thy blood I have,
>   And spotless love and peace.

While they sang the refining fire came down and went through my heart, searching, melting, burning, filling all its chambers with light, and hallowing my whole heart to

God. Oh, the indescribable sweetness of that moment! All words fail to express the blessedness of the spiritual manifestation of Jesus as my Saviour from all sin. My heart warms as I write at the remembrance of the event which transcends all others in my religious history. It was not so much ecstatic emotion I experienced as an unspeakable peace; 'God's love swallowed me up.' For a few moments, ' all its waves and billows rolled over me '. So much afraid was I lest I should lose the delightful sense of the Saviour's presence, that I wished those with me not to speak or disturb me; I wanted to dwell in silence, as my heart was filled with love and gratitude to God.

I need not say the reception of this grace proved an era in my religious life. Many beautiful years have passed away since then. But no words can ever express the complete satisfaction I have in Christ; the sweet sense of rest in His hallowing presence from all worry and care, the ease and joy of His service; not 'I must' now, but 'I may'; the delight I find in prayer and praise; the increased preciousness and fullness of meaning I see in the Scriptures, and the clear and indubitable witness of cleansing through the blood of Jesus. How I wish I could tell of the sweetness, the richness, and indescribable blessedness of this life of perfect love. I cannot tell the story; but I cannot let it alone. O, for a thousand tongues to proclaim Jesus to men, the mighty Saviour, who is able to save them to the uttermost who come unto God by Him! Reader, will you join us and help us to spread the sacred flame?

Printed in Great Britain by
& Warwick (Bedford) Ltd., Harpur Printing Works, Bedford.

Made in the USA
Columbia, SC
23 December 2021

52669467R00100